C000302149

"*Habits of Success* is one of those rare books that successfully manages to distil a wealth of research into an accessible and practical guide for every teacher. The key issues, behaviours and habits that emerge in most busy classrooms are depicted with unerring accuracy and precision. The book goes on to perform the feat of offering evidence-informed approaches to help solve so many of the complex issues facing teachers and their pupils. I seldom make this claim for a book about teaching, but *Habits of Success* could prove to have a transformative impact on those school teachers and leaders who read it and apply its intelligent insights."

Alex Quigley, Education Endowment Foundation

"Being a closet Economics graduate, the concept of nudging has always fascinated me. Books by Kahneman and Thaler are among my non-fiction favourites, and I have regularly tried (and failed) to apply their techniques to get my wife to make my tea and my 2-year-old to sleep through the night. But one thing I had never considered was how these ideas could be applied in the classroom. Step forward Harry Fletcher-Wood. As he displayed in *Responsive Teaching*, Harry has an enviable knack of making complex ideas entirely comprehensible. Here Harry tackles the big questions, questions such as 'How can we convince students to learn?' and 'How can we help students to start?' Through the use of dialogue, readers are able to see exactly how scenarios might play out in the classroom, making this one of the most practical and actionable books I have ever read. A big recommend from me."

Craig Barton, Author of *How I Wish I'd Taught Maths* and
Reflect, Expect, Check, Explain

"*Habits of Success* is clear, well organised and full of useful advice. It embraces . . . research often overlooked but deeply and profoundly meaningful. What you get from Harry is not just the research and interpretation but deep insight and humanity in thinking about how it fits together and what it means. There couldn't be a better guide."

Doug Lemov, Author of *Teach Like a Champion*, *Reading Reconsidered*
and *Coach's Guide to Teaching*

HABITS OF SUCCESS

For students to benefit from lessons, they must attend, listen and try their best. But at times, almost all teachers struggle to manage classroom behaviour and to motivate students to learn. Drawing on decades of research on behavioural science, this book offers teachers practical strategies to get students learning. The key is students' habits. This book reveals simple yet powerful ways to help students build habits of success.

Harry Fletcher-Wood shows how teachers can use behavioural science techniques to increase motivation and improve behaviour. He offers clear guidance on topics such as using role models to motivate students, making detailed plans to help students act and building habits to ensure students keep going. The book addresses five challenges teachers face in encouraging desirable behaviour:

- Choosing what change to prioritise
- Convincing students to change
- Encouraging students to commit to a plan
- Making starting easy
- Ensuring students keep going

Workshops, checklists and real-life examples illustrate how these ideas work in the classroom and make the book a resource to revisit and share. Distilling the evidence into clear principles, this innovative book is a valuable resource for new and experienced teachers alike.

Harry Fletcher-Wood is a teacher, researcher and teacher educator. He has worked in England, Japan, India and Sweden, and is fascinated by making things better and the social, psychological and structural changes this requires. He leads the Teacher Education Fellows programme at Ambition Institute.

HABITS OF SUCCESS

Getting Every Student Learning

Harry Fletcher-Wood

Routledge
Taylor & Francis Group

LONDON AND NEW YORK

First published 2022
by Routledge
2 Park Square, Milton Park, Abingdon, Oxon OX14 4RN

and by Routledge
52 Vanderbilt Avenue, New York, NY 10017

Routledge is an imprint of the Taylor & Francis Group, an informa business

© 2022 Harry Fletcher-Wood

The right of Harry Fletcher-Wood to be identified as author of this work has
been asserted by him in accordance with sections 77 and 78 of the Copyright,
Designs and Patents Act 1988.

All rights reserved. No part of this book may be reprinted or reproduced or
utilised in any form or by any electronic, mechanical, or other means, now
known or hereafter invented, including photocopying and recording, or in any
information storage or retrieval system, without permission in writing from the
publishers.

Trademark notice: Product or corporate names may be trademarks or
registered trademarks, and are used only for identification and explanation
without intent to infringe.

British Library Cataloguing-in-Publication Data
A catalogue record for this book is available from the British Library

Library of Congress Cataloging-in-Publication Data
Names: Fletcher-Wood, Harry, author.
Title: Habits of success : getting every student learning / Harry Fletcher-Wood.
Description: Abingdon, Oxon ; New York, NY : Routledge, 2022. | Includes
     bibliographical references. |
Identifiers: LCCN 2021003402 | ISBN 9780367444945 (hardback) |
     ISBN 9780367444952 (paperback) | ISBN 9781003010067 (ebook)
Subjects: LCSH: Motivation in education. | Effective teaching. | Classroom
     management. | Academic achievement.
Classification: LCC LB1065 .F62 2022 | DDC 370.15/4–dc23
LC record available at https://lccn.loc.gov/2021003402

ISBN: 978-0-367-44494-5 (hbk)
ISBN: 978-0-367-44495-2 (pbk)
ISBN: 978-1-003-01006-7 (ebk)

Typeset in Interstate
by Apex CoVantage, LLC
Printed and bound by CPI Group (UK) Ltd, Croydon, CRO 4YY

Visit the companion website: www.routledge.com/cw/fletcher-
wood

For Daniel

CONTENTS

"Education is mandatory but learning is not."

Mary Kennedy

ACKNOWLEDGEMENTS

Many, many friends and colleagues have improved this book.

Thoughtful critique from Daisy Christodoulou, Josh Goodrich, Jenny Griffiths and Michael Pershan led me to rewrite important sections.

Many early readers offered valuable feedback: the book was particularly improved thanks to comments from Amir Arezoo, Brendan Bayew, Paul Cline, Dan Cronin, Andrew Day, Rachel Ernst, John Etty, Iain Garioch, Peter Hall, Sara Hjelm, James McKenna, Cathy Potter, Josh Powell, Rachel Rossiter, Dave Ruddle, Dom Shibli, Craig Simpson, Sam Thomas, Laura Watkin, Henry Wiggins, Miles Winter and Nick Ye Myint. Routledge's anonymous reviewers also offered exacting and encouraging comments.

Working with Ambition Institute's Teacher Education Fellows to apply these strategies taught me a lot about how to make them work. Feedback from a few Fellows particularly influenced the final draft: thank you Ben Bignall, Jen Calvert, Sarah Cottingham, Alex Douglas, Gemma Edgcome, Susie Fraser, Belinda Goodship, Emma McCrea, Lucy Newman and Ashley Weatherhogg.

Discussing classroom challenges and solutions with a number of teachers shaped crucial aspects of the book: thank you to Janice Allen, Jess Dumbreck, Adele Finch, Lucy Hall, Peter Hall, David Hibbert, Emma Holness, Ollie Lovell, Joel Mendes, Helen Pritchard, Ellie Russell, Dom Shibli, and others who have chosen to remain nameless.

Other teachers suggested ways to tackle specific classroom dilemmas, many of which made their way into the book: thank you to Alice, Charlotte Bell, Paul James, Niki Kaiser, Alice Lane, Steve Lawley, Kate Mason, Amanda Melton, Adam Robbins, Julian Selman, Carrie Swan and E. Wilson.

Valuable suggestions and ideas came from Raj Chande, Peps McCrea and Ben Piper.

I'm very grateful, again, for the support and patience of Annamarie Kino and Amy Welmers at Routledge.

My son was born a few months after I began working on this book. He has tried to contribute to the manuscript, but none of his suggestions survived the editing process. My biggest thanks go to Loren, for her support, and for spending more time than I like to think about looking after Daniel: without her, this book would never have been completed.

Introduction

How can we get every student learning?

Chapter map: introduction

Getting every student learning is hard

We try to get every student learning through:

- Reasoning
- Rewards and punishments
- Making change easy and tempting
- Promoting habits

We can combine these to create habits of success

We learn how to get students learning through trial and error, tips and tricks, and observing others: this is slow and frustrating

We can apply behavioural science to get students learning

I've tried to make this book usable through:
- A focus on challenges
- A clear framework
- Practical examples
- Quick reference resources

What I'm not saying …

Examining our impact matters

"Why are you late?" An everyday example.

Copyright material from Harry Fletcher-Wood (2022), *Habits of Success: Getting Every Student Learning*, Routledge

Why this book?

As a new teacher, I struggled to get my students to learn. If they were to benefit from lessons, I needed them to attend, to listen, and to try their best. Some did. Yet I struggled in every lesson: sometimes with a few students, sometimes with the majority. My Sixth Form tutees arrived late. Many of my Year 10 class refused to listen or work: they said they didn't want to study history. My Year 7 classes seemed enthusiastic, but some students were already struggling to complete relatively simple tasks. I tried to convince students that they should try, that I could help, that the lesson was worthwhile. I tried to promote positive behaviour and enforce basic standards. I tried, but for too many students, I failed. My planning and assessment improved, but many of my students did not benefit.

> *I struggled to get my students to learn*

A universal challenge underlies these individual experiences: most teachers struggle to get all their students learning. One in three teachers report that teaching and learning "largely stopped because of poor behaviour" at some point in the final lesson of the day.[1] Schools vary, but not enormously: half of teachers in poorer areas expected behaviour to affect learning significantly in their next lesson; so did a third of teachers in wealthier areas.[2] Teachers in primary and secondary schools report similar amounts of disruption,[3] and while new teachers struggle most, poor behaviour stopped learning for one in five teachers with *twenty years' experience*.[4] As one researcher has concluded:

> *To some degree*, pupil behaviour and disengagement from learning are problems in nearly all schools, and the questions of how to motivate pupils to want to learn, and how to get a calm, purposeful and collaborative working atmosphere in all classrooms, and stop some pupils spoiling the learning of others are relevant to large numbers of teachers.[5]

Yet creating a calm, purposeful atmosphere is just the foundation: we want students to learn independently, not just follow instructions. And we want diligent and dedicated students to change too, even if it's just to put themselves under less pressure.

> *All teachers struggle, to some extent, to get students to learn*

This book is designed to help you get students learning better, whether you are the struggling new teacher I was, or an experienced teacher or leader. Getting this right matters: poor behaviour holds individuals back, disrupts lessons, and grinds teachers down. Yet while we increasingly apply the science of learning to our planning, we learn to manage and motivate students by watching others, sharing ideas, and painstaking trial and error. There is a science of behaviour, just as there is a science of learning. This book describes what it reveals, offering practical strategies to get every student learning.

> *This book applies behavioural science to get every student learning*

Four approaches to getting students learning

1) Reasoning and experimentation

I began by trying to convince my students that learning mattered. I spent hours explaining the value of studying history, of specific topics, of working hard. I adapted the curriculum around students' interests and experiences. I experimented: with posters encouraging learning, with displaying the names of student "role models of the week," with letting students discover the answers for themselves. Some things worked: students appreciated being named "role model of the week," for example. Some were less effective: Year 8 managed one brilliant self-directed lesson, but never repeated this success. I exhausted myself. Perhaps I changed the opinions of a few students. I don't regret my attempts: I still believe we should show students why learning is worthwhile. But my experiments and attempts at persuasion did not create an orderly classroom, let alone inspire every student.

> *Reasoning may help, but it's not enough*

2) Punishment and reward

When my patience, enthusiasm and imagination ran out, I resorted to punishment and reward. As an idealistic new teacher, I hoped to avoid them: I believed I could persuade all my students to learn. Instead, I found myself telling students off, keeping them in, and giving detentions. Meanwhile, I rewarded those who behaved well: praising them, calling their parents or telling their tutors. This worked – to an extent – but gaining students' cooperation proved exhausting. For example, I got all my Year 8 class to do their homework each week, but only by checking it in the lesson (interrupting teaching) and keeping students in if they hadn't done it: I couldn't do this with every class. My approach also proved emotionally exhausting: it created conflict and resentment, and made future lessons harder. Rewards and punishments can help, but they're hard to sustain: they're not enough to get every student learning.

> *Rewards and punishments help, but they're not enough*

3) Nudges and social influence

The first book I read about behavioural science – *Switch: How to change things when change is hard* – opened my eyes to a more nuanced view of human behaviour.[6] The authors argue that we tend to see resistance to change as a "people problem"; we respond by blaming, cajoling and punishing individuals.[7] (This is what I'd done: I tried to persuade students to act, rewarded them if they did, punished them if they didn't.) Often, however, people want to do something, but are discouraged by the situation and their emotions. For example, a case study in *Switch* asked the reader how to get more employees to submit expense claims on time.[8] My first thought was to enforce the deadline: don't reimburse people who submit claims late. This would encourage prompt submission, but it wouldn't address the underlying problem (people not submitting claims promptly) and it could foster resentment. By contrast, the authors suggested:

- Emphasising that most employees are submitting their expenses on time (encouraging others to follow the norm)
- Identifying how employees who submit promptly are doing it (do they have short-cuts?)
- Emphasising that a colleague must process their claims (appealing to social bonds).[9]

Switch showed me that persuasion and enforcement aren't always enough to overcome obstacles and emotions: I learned to make change easier and more tempting. For example, on a university visit, I'd been talking to a student about an issue they had with a friend. Later, I noticed she was still preoccupied, and was getting nothing from the seminar. Previously, I'd have asked her to "Focus": she might have wanted to, but she would have struggled. Instead, I gave her a simple task which redirected her attention: I asked her to ask a brilliant question before the end of the session. "What, now?" she asked. "Yes!" A few seconds later, her face lit up and her hand flew up. Making change easier and more tempting helped me get students learning – but the effects didn't always last.

> *Nudging students – by making change easy and tempting – helps*

4) Building habits

When I discuss getting students learning, teachers most often ask "How can I motivate my students to learn?" and "How can I get students to manage their own learning?" Increasingly, I've come to believe a third question is more important: how can I help students form good habits?

Motivation

Trying to motivate students seems logical. Bored students try less and do worse[10] (and students say they are bored much of the time).[11] But motivating every student – every lesson – is impossible. First, a student is not "motivated" in general, but motivated by specific things: Alex loves writing stories; Abdi enjoys discussion tasks; Anna likes mathematical puzzles. Few tasks (or topics) will truly motivate them all. Second, motivation fluctuates: it wanes when students tire, or struggle, or see something more tempting. We hope that motivating students will get them learning. But while high-achieving students tend to be more motivated, that doesn't mean motivation caused their success. In fact, researchers find the opposite: when students succeed in maths, their motivation grows (but not the other way around); if they read well, they choose to read more (but not the other way around).[12] (Pursuing motivation may also tempt us to choose easier and more enjoyable tasks and topics, neglecting more rewarding, but more challenging, alternatives.) I'm not saying we shouldn't try to motivate students at all: they must be willing to begin (we discuss ways to motivate students at length in Chapter 2). But motivation is fickle and transient: it's not the secret of students' success, and pursuing it will not get every student learning. The best goal (and the best motivator) is learning itself.

> *Motivation helps, but it's better to pursue student success*

Self-regulation

Similarly, self-regulation helps students learn: they are more likely to succeed if they are able to choose how to approach a task, monitor their progress and adapt accordingly.[13] But, self-regulation is hard. Imagine a student who is struggling to focus, or has chosen an unhelpful strategy to solve a problem. To self-regulate, they must:

- Remember to pause and review what they are doing
- Realise that their current approach isn't working
- Choose a better approach
- Implement that approach.

This imposes high cognitive load: students must simultaneously complete the task and monitor their actions. It also demands substantial expertise: students must know their approach (and the alternatives) well if they are to notice problems and choose better options.[14] In other words, to self-regulate effectively, students must already be fairly successful. Self-regulation is valuable, but student success is our priority. How can we ensure it?

> *Self-regulation is hard: students must already know what they're doing*

Habits: the key to success

Productive habits help students sustain success. A habit is an automatic response to a situation. A student is acting habitually if they always start a sentence with a capital letter, always do homework the day they get it, or always check their working when they finish a problem. This automaticity distinguishes habits from motivated or self-regulated actions. A student could check their working because they want to do well, or because they're trying to monitor their learning better (either would be acceptable). But when they form a habit, they check their working automatically: they no longer have to decide, or be motivated, to do it. Motivation is fickle, self-regulation is effortful: we can't rely on either to get students learning consistently. We can rely on habits: if students check their working automatically, they'll do it even when they're tired, even when they're working independently, and even when they're under pressure in an exam. Habits get – and keep – students learning.[15]

> *Productive habits are the surest way to get – and keep – students learning*

We will have much more to say about the power of habit, what makes a good habit, and how to ensure habits stick; here I want only to introduce two further justifications for pursuing them. First, habits help students focus their efforts, without creating automata. If students plan habitually, they can focus on writing an original and insightful plan (rather than focusing on what to do and whether they are motivated and confident to begin). Second, much of students' daily behaviour (and everyone else's) is already habitual:[16] students face similar situations each day, and their responses become increasingly automatic. This may be positive – "When I get stuck I always ask for help" – or negative: "When I get stuck I give up." Some students come to school with productive habits, but no student is perfect, and some arrive with habits which undermine their success. We may feel uncomfortable planning to influence students' habits, but if we don't, we abandon them to their existing habits: in effect, we renounce our influence on their learning. Helping students form good habits is crucial to getting them learning.

> *Students' success depends on their habits*

Drawing this together

Jonathan Haidt offers the arresting image of a restaurant failing to satisfy because it serves only sweet, or only salty, food.[17] Similarly, we are unlikely to get all students learning if we use only one or two of the approaches described above:

- Reasoning sways some students – but not all.
- Rewards and punishments can be powerful – but they are hard work and can evoke resentment.
- Making change easy and tempting helps – but the effects may not last.
- Motivation and self-regulation are valuable – but pursuing them may not get students learning.
- Habits promise lasting change – but to form habits, we may need to make change easier and to motivate, reward or reason with students.[18]
- We can help students see themselves differently (encouraging further change) – but it's easiest to do this once they are succeeding.

Just as a satisfying meal combines many flavours, to get every student learning we must combine these approaches.[19] This book offers strategies to encourage students, to make change easier, and to make change stick. We can use them separately (we can make a task easier without promoting a habit, for example), but lasting impact is most likely if we combine these approaches to help students form habits of success.

> *We can get all students learning by combining these approaches to help students form habits of success*

What this book offers

Behavioural scientists study habit, motivation and choice, but little of this research reaches teachers.[20] Instead, we learn to manage classrooms and motivate students through trial and error, tips from colleagues, and observing peers. Trial and error is slow and risky: it's hard to regain respect once we've lost it. Tips can be overly prescriptive – "Greet students at the door" – or excessively vague: "Be firm but fair." Observations rarely reveal why colleagues are succeeding: it often looks like force of personality and weight of experience. Craft wisdom is powerful, but this book seeks to move beyond it, by offering practical guidance based on the science of human behaviour.

Critics have suggested behavioural science conveys wisdom your grandmother (or in this case, a more experienced teacher) could have told you.[21] But this wisdom is not always usable. At worst, struggling teachers are offered truisms without concrete guidance: "relationships are crucial" or "culture matters." Behavioural science takes these truisms, tests them, and explains the mechanisms at work. Relationships are crucial; researchers show how to strengthen them (identifying things people have in common, for example). Culture matters; researchers show how it develops through collective traditions. If ideas in this book are familiar, that's encouraging: research should tally with experience. But examining the underlying evidence should make familiar ideas more comprehensible and allow you to use them in new ways (reducing the need for trial and error).

> *Behavioural science allows us to go beyond trial and error, and tips and tricks, to understand what influences students*

The evidence

Behavioural science reveals what drives people's actions. Researchers have applied it to encourage exercise, vaccination, and saving for a pension – among other things – and, in schools, to encourage effort through rewards, reminders and role models. Compared to other disciplines, however, schools have been neglected by researchers.[22] We might conclude that behavioural science offers little – at least until researchers study students like ours, in schools like ours. But research is valuable because it reveals principles we can apply, not because it provides a blueprint which has been tested in every context.[23] Where we lack evidence from schools therefore, I've drawn on research conducted elsewhere: in universities, gyms, hospitals and businesses. Does this apply to our students? Researchers consistently find (for example) that people are more likely to do something if they plan when to do it.[24] It must be worth trying this with our students. Children are not adults, but like adults, they form habits, forget things, and admire role models. (Like adults, but more so, children follow their peers, and prefer immediate rewards to delayed ones.)[25] We can wish for more research in classrooms like ours. Until it takes place, I believe it's better to cautiously apply what we know about human behaviour, than to feign ignorance.

> *Better to apply what we know than to pretend we know nothing*

The reliability of social science research has been challenged. Researchers have struggled to replicate famous research findings: they have repeated the original experiments, but reached different conclusions.[26] While failures to replicate findings are troubling, the exposure of this issue is encouraging: it shows science is weeding out weaker findings; "behaving as it should."[27] Moreover, findings which seemed more robust initially have been replicated successfully.[28] I've used the most robust research I've found, drawing on recent work, meta-analyses and randomised controlled trials where they exist, and expressing doubt where it exists. I've omitted phenomena under dispute, and will post any significant new findings on my blog, improvingteaching.co.uk. As my goal has been to create a usable guide (not an academic treatise), I have discussed research methods only where doing so clarifies the study's import: interested readers are invited to consult the references, and to get in touch.

> *I've drawn on the most robust research available*

A usable guide

I've tried to make this book usable, by:

Organising the book around challenges

The book is organised around five challenges:

- Deciding what to change (Chapter 1)
- Convincing students to act (Chapter 2)
- Getting students to commit to action (Chapter 3)
- Helping students begin (Chapter 4)
- Ensuring students keep going (Chapter 5).

Usually, we need to tackle these in sequence. However, if your students are committed to action but struggling to begin (for example), you may want to skip to Chapter 4. If they still struggle, it's worth revisiting their commitments, their motives, and the change itself. (Where should I start? on page 13 may help you choose where to begin). I've focused on promoting desired improvements because, while we may need to discourage undesirable behaviour (discussed in Chapter 6), our goal is almost always to get students to do something they're not yet doing: to stop shouting out, but also to focus on the lesson. Finally, Chapter 7 discusses ways to encourage teachers to change.

Each chapter breaks a challenge into specific barriers: if we want students to begin, for example, one barrier is lack of confidence. Rather than trying to identify which strategy from the book is most powerful, I would suggest choosing the barrier which seems most acute, and trying to overcome it. Changing many things at once is difficult and yields diminishing returns:[29] it's better to tackle just one or two barriers at a time.

Developing a framework

I've tried to make the framework memorable with a mnemonic; we can SIMPLIFy change if we:

- **S**pecify the change: pick a priority, then choose a powerful habit or small step to achieve it
- **I**nspire and **M**otivate students to value the change
- **PL**an change: ask students to commit to action
- **I**nitiate action: make starting easy
- **F**ollow up: help students keep going.

Offering practical examples

While writing the book, I've invited teachers to discuss how behavioural science can address their challenges. I've included some of the situations we discussed in the "Applications" sections running through each chapter, and in the workshops at the end of the chapter. These are not meant to reflect a perfect cross-section of schools, but I hope they offer relatable examples.

Providing quick references

I've tried to make it easy to use and reuse the book, by including:

- Chapter maps, illustrating the thread of ideas
- Summaries of important points throughout the text
- Key ideas sections, encouraging you to consider how strategies apply in your school
- Checklists summarising the key points (you can also download these at improvingteach ing.co.uk).

I'm not suggesting . . .

. . . that school culture isn't important

A collective approach – across the year team, department or school – makes it easier to get students learning. Students will form habits more quickly, for example, if every teacher expects them to start work immediately, to contribute, and to treat one another respectfully. Most examples in the book describe individual teachers' actions however, for two reasons. First, most teachers report meaningful autonomy over classroom practice:[30] we can change our entry routine, or ask students to plan when to do homework, tomorrow. School policy, on the other hand, is outside our immediate control, and changing it takes longer. Second, classroom examples demonstrate principles which can easily be applied at a larger scale: we can highlight social norms with a class, a year group, or the entire school.

> *School culture is crucial, but I've focused on classroom applications to make the principles clear and usable*

. . . that this solves everything for every student

A student may struggle in school due to learning difficulties, their mental health, or their home environment. They may need specialist help – help which is beyond the classroom teacher's training and beyond the scope of this book. Knowing a student's needs however, the classroom teacher is often forced to decide "What do I do now?" This is the question I have tried to answer. All students – all people – are more likely to act if they have a clear goal, if they form a habit, and if they know their peers are acting. (In some cases, struggling students may benefit most: making a plan particularly helps people with limited self-control, for example.)[31] This book does not pretend to replace specialist support; it will, I hope, help to get all students learning better.

> This book answers "What now?"

... a return to behaviourism

A behaviourist rewards desirable behaviour and punishes undesirable behaviour, until the desirable behaviour sticks (you may have trained a pet using this approach). Behavioural science differs in two important ways. First, behavioural scientists try to understand the complex combination of influences on people's actions: these include rewards and punishments, but also peers, emotions and aspirations. I'm suggesting making learning easy, natural and tempting, not issuing more detentions. Second, a behaviourist decides what the learner is to do – the learner's choices are of little importance. Behavioural scientists try to influence students, but they emphasise helping them make better choices (not forcing them to do things).[32] Indeed, behavioural scientists advocate teaching people behavioural science, helping them to understand their behaviour, and better direct their lives.[33] Behavioural science helps people make better choices, and recognises the complex emotions and motivations influencing those choices: it goes far beyond behaviourism.

> *Behavioural science goes far beyond behaviourism*

Checking our impact

Often, similar people respond to an experiment in different ways. For example, experimenters have found that:

- Encouraging gym attendance using audiobooks influenced busier students more than less busy students.[34]
- Encouraging gym attendance with money led infrequent attendees to go more, but regular attendees went slightly less.[35]
- Hearing about successful graduates inspired new students, but discouraged older ones.[36]

We can't assume the results of our strategies will be straightforward: we must track their impact. We examine how to do this in Chapter 5.

> *We must check the impact of our approach*

An example

Sitting in a school reception, I looked up as a student arrived – "Morning." The teacher asked why he was late.

"I woke up late."
"How's your toe?"
"Feels numb, but better."
"OK, good, have a good day."

There's nothing wrong with this conversation: no doubt there were thousands of similar conversations that morning. But it felt like a missed opportunity to increase the chance of the student arriving on time the next day. The teacher might have:

- Elicited a commitment: "What time will you arrive tomorrow?"
- Prepared a prompt: "Can you set your alarm for tomorrow now?"
- Emphasised a social norm: "Your tutor group were all on time, I'd like you to be with them tomorrow."

(Senior leaders might have worked with teachers to encourage students to build good habits.) This wouldn't have to mean working harder: the teacher was having the conversation already. Nor would it offer a perfect solution. But it might make a small difference, and these differences add up across years, year groups and schools. I hope this book will help you make those small differences add up, to get every student learning.

To share this introduction with a colleague, go to improvingteaching.co.uk/habits/share

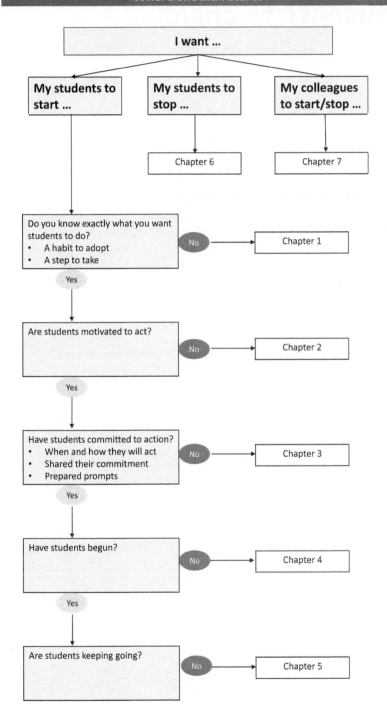

Where should I start?

I want ...

- **My students to start ...**
- **My students to stop ...** → Chapter 6
- **My colleagues to start/stop ...** → Chapter 7

My students to start ...

Do you know exactly what you want students to do?
- A habit to adopt
- A step to take

→ No → Chapter 1

↓ Yes

Are students motivated to act?

→ No → Chapter 2

↓ Yes

Have students committed to action?
- When and how they will act
- Shared their commitment
- Prepared prompts

→ No → Chapter 3

↓ Yes

Have students begun?

→ No → Chapter 4

↓ Yes

Are students keeping going?

→ No → Chapter 5

Copyright material from Harry Fletcher-Wood (2022), *Habits of Success: Getting Every Student Learning*, Routledge

1 What should we ask students to change?

> **Specify the change: pick a priority, then choose a powerful habit or small step to achieve it**
>
> Inspire and motivate students to value the change
>
> PLan change: ask students to commit to action
>
> Initiate action: make starting easy
>
> Follow up: help students keep going

Chapter map: what should we ask students to change?

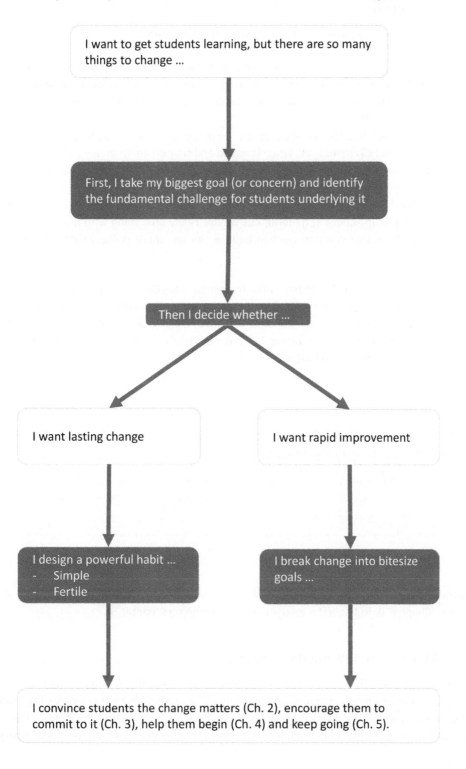

I want to get students learning, but there are so many things to change …

First, I take my biggest goal (or concern) and identify the fundamental challenge for students underlying it

Then I decide whether …

I want lasting change

I want rapid improvement

I design a powerful habit …
-   Simple
-   Fertile

I break change into bitesize goals …

I convince students the change matters (Ch. 2), encourage them to commit to it (Ch. 3), help them begin (Ch. 4) and keep going (Ch. 5).

Copyright material from Harry Fletcher-Wood (2022), *Habits of Success: Getting Every Student Learning*, Routledge

The problem

All our students could be doing something better. For example:

- Ellie Russell describes Joe, in her Year 11 Science class, as "bright, but often lazy." He "regularly distracts peers and disrupts lessons. He wants attention from peers or me all the time: he's equally happy to get negative or positive attention, as long as it is attention."
- Adele Finch has four pupils who are "reluctant to break words into chunks and sounds to help them spell. When I remind and support them to use a phonics mat and to segment words their spellings are accurate. Without support and reminders their spelling for 'children' looks like 'chren.'"
- Richard is worried about "whole-school apathy . . . We have cracked the serious disruption in school in general, but we are really struggling with our students' attitude to learning. We want to build a culture where doing your best is the norm."

How to get each student learning – what to change – may be less obvious than it seems however. For example, Ellie needs Joe to work harder, demand less attention and be less distracting: where should she start and what, exactly, should she ask him to do? We may want to change everything, but this would devour our time and dissipate our energy: what should we prioritise?

The principle: specify the change

To get students learning, we must first specify what we want them to do. This means prioritising the most fundamental challenge, then choosing a powerful habit or a bite-size step which addresses it.

Specifying the change should make it easier to convince students to act (Chapter 2), to plan action (Chapter 3), to begin (Chapter 4) and to keep going (Chapter 5).

1.1 If there are many things to change

There may be many things we would like students to do differently. Trying to change them all at once would be exhausting however, and likely unsuccessful: we must prioritise. For example, we may want Sofia to focus better, contribute more and structure answers more clearly – but we can neither expect nor support her to do all three at once. Instead, we need to begin with the most fundamental step: the change which makes other changes possible. This is easier with a sequence of steps in mind. For example, if students are to learn, they must:

1)   Focus on learning and avoid distractions
2)   Approach tasks using appropriate techniques
3)   Persevere, with increasing independence
4)   Contribute, speaking in discussions and helping one another, for example.

Separating these challenges may seem artificial: we can help students focus by reminding them about the technique; we can encourage them to persevere and to contribute in the same breath. However, a student can overcome each challenge only if they have mastered the preceding ones: if Sofia knows how to structure her answer, but isn't focusing, she will achieve nothing; if she perseveres, but doesn't know what structure to use, she will learn little; if she hasn't tried, she can contribute little. If we want to make several changes, we must begin with the most fundamental.[37]

> *We can get students learning by prioritising the most fundamental challenge they face: success makes further improvements possible*

The strategies described in this book can be used to help students do anything, including completing their homework, applying to university, avoiding conflict with peers, and getting a good night's sleep. Whatever the goal, we are most likely to succeed if we take our biggest concern and identify the fundamental challenge underlying it. First, we pick an issue: Jack keeps calling out; students aren't finishing their work. Then, we identify the underlying challenge: Jack isn't focused; students are using inappropriate techniques. We could use the sequence suggested in the previous paragraph, but the crucial point is not the sequence itself, but the idea of sequencing – of ensuring we prioritise the first step towards improvement, not just the most obvious issue. This may be subject-specific: do students grasp the play's outline well enough to analyse it? It may be physical: does students' posture support them to form their letters properly? It may be social: are students listening before they comment? We may feel unsure whether the challenge we have chosen is the right one. If so, we could ask colleagues, or just try addressing it: if students attempt to change, but struggle to improve, we may need to pick something more fundamental. Whatever we want to change, we must take what concerns us and identify the fundamental challenge: the first step towards improvement.

> *We can prioritise by taking a concern and identifying the first step towards improvement*

Applications

- Joe isn't working hard enough and is distracting peers. He knows what to do and needs no encouragement to contribute; the challenge is getting him to focus.
- Adele wants her pupils to break words down. The problem isn't focus – the children aren't distracted or demotivated – it's ensuring they apply the appropriate technique.
- Richard wants to build a culture where "doing your best is the norm." His students are willing to focus and know what techniques to use; he needs them to persevere.

By targeting the fundamental challenge, Ellie, Adele and Richard can go beyond immediate frustrations, like disruption or lack of effort, to lay foundations for success: getting students focused on learning, not just sitting quietly; encouraging perseverance, not just occasional effort. Success makes further improvement possible: once Joe focuses, Ellie can help him select effective techniques; once Richard's students persevere, their contributions will be more valuable.

Key idea

Usually we know roughly what needs to change. But we struggle to narrow our focus to a priority (and to let other important things go in order to achieve it). Change is hard and, as we'll see in the next section, students form habits slowly. We cannot change everything: we must prioritise. We can do so by asking ourselves:

1)   What do I most want for students? What is concerning me most?
2)   What is the fundamental challenge? What is the first step towards improvement?

We must address the fundamental challenge before tackling other issues.

Having prioritised a challenge, we can overcome it by helping students form a powerful habit, or take a small step.

1.2 If we want students to make a lasting change

Students often make isolated improvements: they have a better lesson, or a better week. But isolated improvements don't bring about consistent success. To do their homework – once – a student must want to do it, plan to do it, and stick to their plan. This kind of self-control is hard:[38] they may succeed sometimes, but their motivation can slip, and their plans can go awry. Imagine, instead, that they start doing their homework on Saturday morning. If someone repeats an action in the same situation for long enough, they form a habit: the situation (in this case, Saturday morning) comes to prompt the action (doing homework).[39] As we discussed in the Introduction, a habit is an *automatic response* to a situation. Having formed a habit, motivation, confidence and planning stop being barriers:[40] Saturday morning prompts them to do their homework, however they feel. This makes habit the key to lasting change. Instead of isolated improvements (requiring fresh motivation, ongoing self-control, and substantial support from us), we need students to form habits of success: to focus whenever they have a task, pick the appropriate technique whenever they see a question, and contribute whenever they have the opportunity.

> *Habits are lasting solutions to fundamental challenges*

Forming new habits is slow and difficult. Existing habits may be a barrier. I mentioned that habits form when people repeat actions in specific situations. Students face some situations frequently – being asked a question, for example. If they respond in similar ways, these become habits – perhaps undesirable ones, like guessing, calling out or giving rambling responses. Existing habits endure, even when people want to change:[41] after a heart bypass, only one patient in ten eats better and exercises more.[42] If adults in mortal danger struggle to eat differently, students who enjoy chatting to their friends will struggle to focus. Moreover, it takes people several weeks' repetition to form even simple new habits, like drinking water with lunch, or going to the gym.[43] It may take students longer if we don't see them frequently. Forming new habits is hard: to justify the time and effort required, the habits we encourage must be powerful.

> *Forming desirable habits is slow and difficult: we must choose powerful habits which are worth this effort*

What makes a habit powerful?

In 1987, Paul O'Neill took over Alcoa, a massive, inefficient aluminium manufacturer. He was under pressure to improve the struggling company rapidly; his predecessor's attempts had caused fifteen thousand workers to strike.[44] Yet O'Neill did not set profit or productivity goals: his aim – the fundamental challenge he set out to solve – was zero worker injures; to make Alcoa "the safest company in America."[45] O'Neill designed a powerful habit to influence the actions of every employee, and the culture of Alcoa: if anyone was injured, the unit manager had to inform O'Neill within twenty-four hours, and present a plan to ensure the injury never happened again.

The habit was powerful because it was both simple and fertile. It was simple because a clear cue demanded concrete, rapid and obvious action: an injury (cue) demanded a report (concrete) within twenty-four hours (rapid) to O'Neill himself (obvious). It was fertile because it encouraged collaboration, flexibility and wider change. It promoted collaboration by giving managers and workers a shared goal: managers had to trust workers to pre-empt risks; workers had to accept more oversight to identify risks. The goal was specific – avoiding injuries – but the means were not: this flexibility allowed workers and managers to identify and act upon the improvements needed. And it promoted wider change, because the apparently simple goal of avoiding injuries meant understanding production, updating machinery and improving communication: it required a "habit of excellence" across the organisation,[46] making Alcoa the "best, most streamlined aluminium company on earth."[47]

Powerful habits create lasting change. At Alcoa, injuries evaporated: twenty years later – after O'Neill's departure – American workers were more likely to be injured working in accountancy, software or animation than handling molten aluminium at Alcoa.[48] It transformed the organisation, cutting costs, improving productivity and returning Alcoa to profit. And it changed people's behaviour: employees described challenging risky behaviour on the street, not just at work. We often seek to change a culture, but sometimes this just means telling students to do something: we see temporary change, then find ourselves nagging them again a week later. A powerful habit is simple enough to stick, and fertile enough to cause meaningful transformation.[49]

> *Powerful habits are simple enough to stick, and fertile enough to cause meaningful transformation*

How to design powerful habits for students

I stumbled on a powerful habit while trying to encourage my A level politics students to read the news regularly. Reading the news would bring the course to life, helping students to grasp abstract concepts, like checks on executive power, and write compelling exam answers. Yet my encouragement and exhortations achieved nothing: some weeks my students couldn't tell me a single recent news story. Eventually, I began setting a weekly quiz: students had to get at least six out of ten right, if they didn't, they had to return with the completed quiz later that week.

This proved a powerful habit: simple and fertile. It was concrete: what students had to do was clear (read the news) and whether they were doing it was obvious (they got at least six out of ten right). It was rapid and frequent: the quiz took ten minutes and ran weekly. It was flexible: I suggested websites, but students were free to choose what to read and when. It promoted collaboration: students worked together to predict news stories on the quiz and to identify the correct answers afterwards if they had struggled. And it catalysed wider change: students read the news regularly, became interested in the stories and used them in their essays; they even started to suggest stories they thought should have been on the quiz (for bonus points). A powerful habit fostered meaningful change.

Applications

We begin with the challenge we have prioritised: Joe demands Ellie's attention constantly; Ellie's priority is helping him focus. First, Ellie can design a simple habit:

1) She might ask Joe to "Focus on your work." This is simple, but there is no clear cue to begin, and it's not clear exactly what Joe should do.
2) She could tell Joe: "Whenever I say, 'Start writing,' I want you to write non-stop until your answer is complete." This gives him a concrete task and a clear cue to begin, but his response could be more obvious.
3) She could tell Joe: "Whenever I say, 'Start writing,' I want you to write non-stop. As soon as you've finished, put your hand up and I'll come and check it." This makes Joe's progress more obvious.

This simple habit should help Joe focus and reduce his demands for attention: he gets attention by writing an answer. Ellie could make the habit more fertile by using it to encourage further change.

4) She could tell Joe: "Whenever I say, 'Start writing,' I want you to write non-stop. When you finish, review the model answer: make sure yours is as good or better. Then, put your hand up and I'll come and check it." This should challenge Joe to create high-quality work before seeking attention.

Joe may struggle to adopt this version of the habit immediately: Ellie may focus initially on getting him writing; once he is writing habitually, she can push him to review and improve his work. Challenges remain: Ellie has to convince Joe (Chapter 2), make starting easy (Chapter 4) and encourage him to keep going (Chapter 5). Nor is this a perfect solution: Joe's wish for attention is still influencing her actions excessively. Nonetheless, this habit should reduce Joe's demands, helping him focus more, disrupt less, and produce better work.

Adele can design a powerful habit to ensure her pupils use the appropriate technique: breaking words into chunks to spell correctly. The action is concrete – "Break words down" – but she can:

- Specify a cue – "Whenever you encounter a word you don't recognise . . ."
- Encourage an immediate response – "your first action is to break it down" and
- Make this response obvious – "then write the word on a sticky note."

Adele can make the habit more fertile by encouraging students to collaborate: "show the word you've sounded out to your partner and check if you're right"; this should encourage all pupils to use the technique, and provide them with feedback on their first attempt. So the powerful habit would be: "Whenever you encounter a word you don't recognise, first break it down, then write the word on a sticky note. Then show the note to a peer to check you're right." She may need to remind students how to break words down, train them to collaborate and encourage them to persevere, but all students should spell better as a result.

Richard can design a powerful habit to encourage students to persevere across lessons. He can set a concrete goal – "Complete all tasks as best you can" – and make students' actions obvious by clarifying that they should either be writing, reviewing their work, or have their hand up waiting for help. He can make the habit more fertile by encouraging students to keep improving – "if you get stuck, review the model" – and asking them to persevere – "keep trying for one more minute before asking for help." So the powerful habit is to "Complete all tasks as best you can: that means you should either be writing, reviewing your work, or have your hand up waiting for help, at all times. If you get stuck, review the model and keep trying for one more minute before asking for help." Encouraging all students to adopt this approach will be challenging, but even partial success should increase students' perseverance significantly.

Key idea

Having chosen a goal, we can design a powerful habit by asking:

- **How can I make the habit simple? Can I offer a clearer cue, or make the action more concrete, obvious, rapid or frequent?**
- **How can I make the habit fertile? Can I offer more flexibility, or encourage collaboration and wider change?**

By asking students to form a powerful habit, we promote lasting, meaningful change. (Ways to help students keep pursuing a habit are discussed in Chapter 5.) Sometimes however, we may want immediate progress: if so, rather than building a habit, we can give students bite-size goals.

1.3 If we want students to make an immediate change

Goals encourage action by focusing people's attention and increasing their interest and effort.[50] Often we set big goals, which are laudable aspirations, but too vague to guide action: we tell students we want them to "Think for themselves," for example. More powerful, however, is a concrete, bitesize goal which clarifies exactly what we want students to do next: people are much more likely to act if they have a clear goal (as opposed to no goal, or a vague goal).[51] Effective goals are challenging but achievable:[52] their immediacy puts them within students' reach. They are also limited: one goal allows students to focus; multiple goals overburden their limited working memory.[53] At each step of a task, students are asking themselves "What do I do next?"[54] Each step is a chance to lose their way, their focus, interest, or confidence. Small goals show students what to do next, helping them to start, and to stay on track. Specific, challenging, achievable goals clarify what students should do next, getting them learning.

Specific, challenging, achievable goals guide and encourage action

---

How to break big tasks into bitesize goals

Setting bitesize goals is hard, because we have to break tasks into surprisingly small steps. Experts automate their actions, losing sight of the individual steps:[55] we no longer think about releasing the clutch or engaging first gear, we just drive to work. This means we forget how hard an action is, and struggle to break it into the smaller steps a novice can hold in their working memory. To set goals, we must break these skills down again. There are two ways to ensure we are setting genuinely bitesize goals:

- **Break tasks down in advance.** We could complete the task, trying to avoid jumping to the answer, and instead asking ourselves "What am I doing and why?" Or we could ask a student to complete the task and describe their thinking. This should give us a series of steps, some of which seem obvious: to help students focus on a task, for example, we may need to specify, "Decide your opening sentence, pick up your pen, start writing, ignore any distractions." To help students pick the right technique to answer a question, we might specify: "First rephrase the question, then identify the focus, then list the possible techniques." Once we've broken the task into steps, we can ask colleagues or students to check if we've missed anything.
- **Break tasks down when students struggle.** When students struggle - stopping, losing focus or choosing the wrong technique - the current goal may be unmanageable. This is a good cue to pause and set a clearer, smaller goal: "I notice some people getting stuck, let's go back to Question 3, remind me the first thing we do when we approach a question like this."

Whenever we simplify and break down tasks, we make it easier for students to respond.[56]

We can break big tasks into bitesize goals by examining the task in advance, or by breaking it down when students struggle

---

I learned the power of bitesize goals while trying to help students write essays. Initially, I simply asked students to "Make a plan before you start writing." After a decade writing history essays, I planned instinctively: I only recognised the need for smaller, clearer steps when

I realised how many students were struggling. I set a series of bitesize goals, based on how I planned and where students got stuck. In my first attempt, the first three goals were:

1)   Choose three topics for your paragraphs - write them as branches of a mind-map.
2)   For each point, write three good bits of evidence.
3)   Get a peer to check your evidence.

This allowed more students to plan and write coherent essays. Nonetheless, some still struggled, because the goals I had chosen were still too big: choosing paragraph topics, for example, requires students to recall what they know, decide what's relevant, and identify themes. A smaller first step - achievable for all students - would be "Write everything you can remember about the question in two minutes"; identifying themes (to form paragraphs) would become the second step.[57] Craig Barton's aim, when introducing a complicated mathematical process to students, is not just to break it down, but to break it into as many steps as possible. For example, he broke solving simultaneous equations into nine steps, beginning:

1)   Decide if the equations are in the correct form.
2)   Decide if we need to manipulate one or both equations.
3)   Decide if we need to add or subtract.[58]

Breaking tasks down allows more students to apply an appropriate technique: the key is to keep breaking it down until the steps are truly achievable.

There are many ways to break learning down. The previous paragraph showed ways to break tasks down, but we could also break lessons into a series of tasks: first learn the key vocabulary, then read the text, then write a response. We could break the time down: instead of asking his Year 9 Business Studies class to focus for an hour, Colin Lee asks for fifteen minutes' focused, independent work, then gives students a three-minute "break" (a discussion task), before the next bitesize goal, thirteen minutes' independent work. We can use bitesize goals to support independent work too: English teacher Josh Goodrich noticed that students revised better on structured, gamified websites, so he broke the English Literature syllabus into hundreds of quiz questions. Finally, effective goals can specify not only tasks - "Write for the next three minutes" - but also outcomes: "Keep practising until you can get them all right."[59] Any aspect of learning can be broken into smaller goals.

We can break time, or tasks, into as many steps as are needed

---

Applications

If Ellie, Adele and Richard want to turn their priorities into bitesize goals:

•   Joe isn't working hard enough and is distracting peers: Ellie could tell him, "I'd like you to write for another minute, without looking up," or "I'd like you to write your

first/next sentence before I come to you." On her return, she could just ask for
another minute's work, or another sentence.

- Adele wants her pupils to break words down: she could tell them to "Identify the
first sound in the word."
- Richard wants to build a culture where "doing your best is the norm": he could ask
every student to "Try for a minute longer whenever you feel stuck," or to "Review
previous examples and try one alternative approach before asking for help."

In each case, the goal is not to solve the whole problem, but to give students a clear
next step.

Key idea

We can help students act by asking:

- **How can I break this task into smaller steps?**
- **Where are students struggling?**
- **What step should they take next?**

**We often believe we have broken a task down enough, but whenever students get
stuck, we need to break it down further.**

The need to break things down is no surprise, but it's worth emphasising. First, because we
can easily underestimate how hard students will find a task which we have mastered. Second,
because bitesize goals help us to encourage action by:

- Creating a sense of urgency: an immediate goal demands action more obviously than an
exam next year.
- Making it easier for students to start: we can reveal one step at a time, making success
seem more achievable.
- Assessing students' progress rapidly: pinpointing barriers and offering support and
encouragement immediately, rather than waiting optimistically.
- Highlighting small wins, showing students they are succeeding.

(We discuss these strategies in detail in Chapters 4 and 5.) Finally, we may avoid breaking
tasks down because we want to challenge students and encourage independence. But small
goals let students master challenges in stages: once they can complete individual steps fluently, we can help them integrate those steps. The more students can master, and combine,
small tasks, the more independent they can be.

Conclusion

To encourage change we must prioritise among our aspirations and challenges, then turn our priority into a powerful habit or bitesize goals. This means asking:

•   What is the most fundamental challenge students face?

Then, if we have time to create lasting change:

•   What powerful habit would help them to overcome it?

Or if we want immediate progress:

•   What smaller steps would help them make progress?

We may revisit these questions many times, as students struggle, or master the changes we ask them to make. Once students are familiar with the process, we may invite them to identify priorities, select habits or break tasks into bitesize goals. However, while a specific priority should encourage students to begin, further persuasion may be needed. This is the subject of the next chapter.

☑ Checklist

I **s**pecify what I want students to do	
1) If there are many things to change, rather than trying to change everything at once, I **prioritise** ...	
I pick my biggest concern and identify the fundamental challenge underlying it. For example, I ask whether students are: 1) Focusing 2) Using the right technique 3) Persevering 4) Contributing	*My students aren't engaging with the lesson. I want them to persevere and contribute, but currently they aren't focusing on independent tasks: that's my priority.*
2) If I want students to make a lasting change, I don't just ask them to act, **I help them form a powerful habit** ...	
Make it simple: • Clear cue • Concrete task • Rapid and frequent action • Obvious	*"When I say, 'Writing time starts now,' I'd like you to write in silence, starting immediately, and put up your hand when finished."*
Make it fertile: • Collaborative • Flexible • Encouraging wider change	*"When you finish, review each other's answers, then choose a hard question and write a model answer together."*
3) If I want students to make an immediate change, I don't just offer big goals, **I break the task into bitesize goals** ...	
Break tasks or time into specific, challenging, bitesize goals.	*"Decide your first sentence, tell your partner, then start writing."*
Next, I **i**nspire and **m**otivate students to change (Chapter 2), help students **pl**an (Chapter 3), initiate (Chapter 4) and **f**ollow up (Chapter 5) change.	

Copyright material from Harry Fletcher-Wood (2022), *Habits of Success: Getting Every Student Learning*, Routledge

Workshop 1: a good start to the lesson

What's the situation?

Mark struggles to get students learning at the start of afternoon lessons. Students drift from the playground in small groups, then rush to the coat hooks and their seats. They are excitable and settling into the first task takes time: Mark finds this frustrating, and sometimes struggles to get the lesson on track. When things go wrong, he reiterates what he wants, but by the next afternoon students seem to have forgotten. Mark is considering lining students up before allowing them in, and issuing sanctions immediately to anyone who doesn't calm down. Jo-Ann, Mark's mentor, is worried that this won't ensure students focus. (This is a situation which many new teachers, and many mentors, face.)

You may want to consider what you would recommend before reading my suggestions:

1)   What is the fundamental challenge? What habit or steps would solve it?
2)   How would you inspire students to act?
3)   Do students need to commit to action?
4)   How can you make it easy?
5)   How can you help students keep going?

Step 1) Specify the change

Jo-Ann wants Mark to see that the goal is for students to start learning rapidly – calming students down is necessary, but not sufficient. Mark's aims are ambitious but vague: he wants to create a "positive, motivating and secure learning environment." She helps Mark to recognise that his fundamental challenge is ensuring all students focus on learning as quickly as possible.

Next, Mark lists everything that students do at the start of a lesson: hanging up coats, collecting books, distributing sheets, checking the board and so on. Jo-Ann helps Mark simplify his list, removing anything which isn't immediately crucial: for example, Mark defers student questions about homework, and has one student distribute books. This leaves Mark with a simple habit for students to follow when they enter the classroom: hang up coats, sit down, equipment out, start the first task.

Jo-Ann wants Mark to go beyond a basic routine and create a powerful habit with ongoing benefits for students. She suggests that a good first task for every lesson would be going back through their books and quizzing themselves on recent topics, putting a star by anything they get wrong. Once Mark has taught them how to do this, it's simple for students to get started: this allows Mark to help latecomers settle. It's also fertile: it should boost students' retention and activate prior knowledge they can apply in the lesson. (Additionally, it shows Mark where students are struggling and gives students a skill they can use more widely.)

Step 2) Inspire and motivate students

Mark highlights the value of the change by discussing the problem: after a disrupted start to a lesson, he asks students to raise their hands if they're feeling calm, and if they think the lesson is going well. Having agreed there is a problem, Mark describes what he wants students to do in future, and emphasises a social norm: other classes have already settled into learning.

Step 3) Plan change

Mark posts a reminder of what students should do by the door, drawing students' attention to it as they enter.

Step 4) Initiate action

Previously, students had to work out what they needed to do at the start of each lesson. By setting a default – the first task is always self-quizzing – Mark reduces the potential for confusion. Jo-Ann encourages him to stick to this default, even if the rest of the lesson will feature something unusual, like a visitor to speak to students. Mark prepares students for the change by rehearsing the new routine during a morning lesson. He gets them to practise entering the room and beginning work immediately; he also demonstrates and practises self-quizzing until he is sure students know how to do it well.

Step 5) Follow up

Jo-Ann emphasises the importance of students feeling they are making progress. Mark times how long it takes students to all be sitting and reviewing, encouraging them to beat their previous time. He notes what's going well as students enter the lesson – "I see Gabriella's already reviewing" – and highlights norms: "almost everybody has started." Jo-Ann suggests emphasising students' progress as he introduces the next task: stopping the review, highlighting what students now know, then asking them to move on to the next – slightly harder – task. Jo-Ann hopes that highlighting students' successes will encourage them to keep going.

Conclusion

Students feel more secure and more settled, and their retention of key ideas improves. Jo-Ann identifies two other ways she can support Mark, although she doesn't mention them to him immediately. First, the routine may slip near the end of term: if it does, Jo-Ann will suggest Mark reminds students about it and its importance. Second, creating norms and routines is challenging for individual teachers: she will suggest to senior leaders that teachers agree a common routine for entering the classroom.

2   How can we convince students to learn?

Specify the change: pick a priority, then choose a powerful habit or small step to achieve it

Inspire and motivate students to value the change

PLan change: ask students to commit to action

Initiate action: make starting easy

Follow up: help students keep going

Chapter map: how can we convince students to learn?

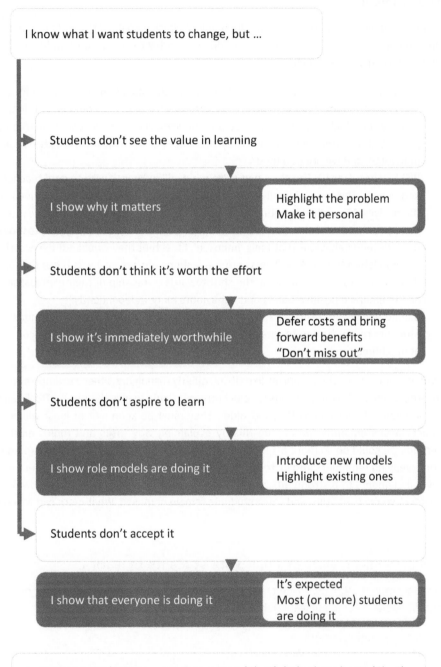

I know what I want students to change, but …

Students don't see the value in learning

I show why it matters | Highlight the problem
Make it personal

Students don't think it's worth the effort

I show it's immediately worthwhile | Defer costs and bring forward benefits
"Don't miss out"

Students don't aspire to learn

I show role models are doing it | Introduce new models
Highlight existing ones

Students don't accept it

I show that everyone is doing it | It's expected
Most (or more) students are doing it

I encourage students to commit to action (Ch. 3), help them begin (Ch. 4) and keep going (Ch. 5).

Copyright material from Harry Fletcher-Wood (2022), *Habits of Success: Getting Every Student Learning*, Routledge

The problem

Chapter 1 suggested choosing a powerful habit or bitesize goal for students to pursue. Once we know what we want students to do, we can try to convince them it's worthwhile. This can be challenging:

- Helen teaches Year 6; she doesn't face behaviour management issues and her pupils are "generally happy individuals," but they seem to be "completely unbothered by their lack of progress," they are "undismayed by poor test scores/badly presented work/repeated errors. They seem neither intrinsically nor extrinsically motivated, and we are at a loss!"
- Will teaches Year 10. The class had a "rough deal" in Year 9, with several teachers and cover. "They were initially very badly behaved and had low expectations of themselves. Through attempting to be as consistent as possible they are now much more positive, and their behaviour has improved. However, I am struggling to move them beyond behaviour that feels 'imposed'. I feel that they would not necessarily be completing the work well, answering questions etc. unless I was there to make them. I want to help them make the shift towards ownership of their own learning and to embrace positive habits and behaviours more independently."
- Janine teaches in a Further Education college and is struggling with attendance. Students resent having to retake English and Maths GCSE, and leave the college at lunchtime.

We can enforce behavioural norms like sitting quietly (usually). As these examples illustrate however, while routines help, we can't force students to give their best effort – and our influence diminishes as they get older. They must be keen – or at least willing – to act. Most frequently, we pursue this by explaining why tasks and topics matter. Perhaps we could do so more often (students may have forgotten our initial explanation), weaving reminders into instructions: "I'd like you to plan first, because there are several elements to a strong answer." If you've chosen to read this chapter, however, I suspect you're doing this, and some students remain unmoved. What more can we do?

The principle: inspire and motivate students to learn

We can motivate students to study a topic (or a subject), or to take an action (a bitesize goal or habit), by communicating its value:

- Demonstrating it matters
- Making it seem immediately worthwhile.

And by emphasising that it's socially desirable:

- Highlighting role models
- Illustrating social norms.

We need not use every strategy or justify every step: we can choose the strategy most likely to convince (knowing our students), the most powerful illustration (an obvious role model, for example), and we can focus on topics and habits of lasting importance.

2.1 If students don't see the value in learning

Students given a neutrally phrased leaflet about tetanus were unmoved; they reacted emotionally (and went to get vaccinated) when the leaflet conveyed the same points through images, vivid language and a description of a patient's experience.[60] Telling students something matters is seldom enough: they must feel that it solves a problem, or matters to them personally.

We can highlight the problem

Recognising a problem inspires people to act. In developing countries, for example, one charity has changed health habits by vividly illustrating a problem: a facilitator shows how flies spread infection, by dipping a hair in waste, then in a glass of water, and asking if anyone is willing to drink the water.[61] Often however, we give students solutions to problems they have never encountered.[62] Maths teacher Dan Meyer suggests seeing ourselves as selling aspirin: we need to induce a headache (to have students experience a problem) before offering the aspirin (what we want them to learn).[63] This need not be a real-world problem: Meyer advocates letting students experience the limits of their existing mathematical knowledge before introducing a new technique.[64] To introduce simplifying fractions, for example, we could ask students to shade 17 of 34 segments of a circle. This can be done without knowing that $\frac{17}{34}$ is a half, but it's inefficient. The headache makes the value of the aspirin clear: it's easier to compare (and draw) simplified fractions.[65] Similarly, we could:

- Cast doubt on students' existing beliefs: "If the king is so powerful, why does he face so many rebellions?"
- Induce confusion: collect competing explanations for what happens to the wax when a candle burns.
- Give challenges which students can't yet complete: ask them to buy a sandwich in French.
- Set up a cliffhanger: begin a story and withhold what happens next.

We can extend this to highlighting the problems a subject solves: doubt about what really happened in the past (history), ignorance about what's happening around the world now (geography) or difficulty expressing ideas clearly and persuasively (literacy/English). Leaving students struggling to solve a problem unguided is usually a mistake: novices learn best from explicit teaching.[66] But a little struggle initially may increase their motivation to learn.

> *Induce a headache, by posing a problem, before offering students the aspirin: what you want them to learn*

Similarly, we can encourage actions by highlighting the problems they address, either through asking students to recall a problem, or through simulating it. To motivate students to keep their work organised, for example, we could ask them to describe a time they couldn't find something important (and how they felt), or ask them to find a recent piece of work and time how long it takes.

To show the value of . . .	We could ask students about a time when they . . .	Or we could simulate the problem by . . .
Focusing	Were too distracted to concentrate	Asking students to work without setting a noise limit, then discussing the impact
Choosing the right technique	Applied the wrong technique to a problem	Giving students an unfamiliar problem without guidance
Persevering	Gave up on a goal, and how it felt	Giving students hard – but achievable – problems
Collaborating	Benefitted from a peer's help	Asking students to record three things they know about a new topic, and compare their lists

Students may not recognise the problem automatically: to change hygiene habits, a trained facilitator needed to highlight the issue. We can prepare follow-up questions – "What causes this? How could we avoid it?" – and answers to potential sceptical responses: "You say talking helps you concentrate, but if you're thinking about the discussion, you're not thinking about your answer." We should spend only as long as it takes to illustrate the problem before introducing the solution: the goal is to induce a headache, not a migraine (nor to undermine classroom routines or relationships). But a mild headache may illustrate that an action matters better than a careful explanation.

> *We can show an action matters by asking students to describe past headaches, or by simulating those headaches*

We can make it personal

Highlight autonomy

Autonomy and choice motivate students[67] – but they can make learning harder. Choosing how to learn demands students' attention, diverting them from the task.[68] Choosing what to learn may mean they miss out on important areas of knowledge, undermining their understanding.[69] And choosing well is hard: students struggle to assess their needs accurately,[70] and often adopt ineffective learning strategies.[71] If students can succeed autonomously, then autonomy may motivate them (and reduce the burden on us). But motivation does not depend upon autonomy: people are just as likely to pursue goals they set as goals others set for them.[72] How goals are set may be as important as who sets them:[73] rather than offering extensive autonomy, we can set the direction and highlight the autonomy it offers. For example, we can set the objective (an essay, for example) and invite students to choose which character to discuss; or explain the task and ask students how long they need. We can also emphasise that the habits and skills we are teaching prepare students for autonomy: "We're going to practise this until you don't need my input at all." And we can emphasise that students already have extensive autonomy: Peter Hall, a maths teacher at Beacon Academy, describes the Ghost of Christmas Yet-To-Come to students, and asks them to choose between arriving promptly and positively, and benefiting from the lesson, or arriving late, unsure and angry. We should be cautious how much autonomy we offer, but we may motivate students by highlighting how much autonomy they have.

> *Set the direction, but highlight the autonomy it offers*

Help students find personal meaning

People like things which seem personal. They respond more readily to personally addressed invitations,[74] and are more willing to save if shown a digitally aged image of their face.[75] Intriguing as these findings are however, they're hard to apply: we can't personalise learning or messages for students regularly. Sometimes however, a generic prompt can make a message feel personal. For example, people who were prompted to "Picture who you'll spend time with in retirement," were more likely to consider planning their pensions.[76] Predicting what will motivate students (and personalising materials accordingly) is hard – but the right prompt may help students see how learning matters to them.[77] For example, explaining the value of a mathematical technique demotivated less confident students (possibly because they felt they'd be unable to apply it).[78] But explaining its value, then asking students to write about how they could use it, increased their interest and their learning. Elsewhere, researchers asked students to explain how learning "would help them be the kind of person they want to be" or "make the kind of impact they want on the people around them or society in general"; one student hoped to use their scientific understanding to "solve our energy problems."[79] As a result, students found science and maths tasks more meaningful, persisted for longer, and gained higher grades. So, having explained why a topic or technique matters, we can ask students what interests them about it, what they hope to achieve or contribute, or who will be proud of their success. Personalising learning is hard, but the right prompt can help students see that learning matters to them.

> *We can prompt students to find personal meaning in learning*

Applications

If Helen, Will and Janine want to show students that change matters:

- Helen's Year 6 class are "undismayed" by poor work. She might highlight the problem poor work poses, for example, by asking pupils to decipher an incoherent text about an interesting subject – perhaps a garbled letter about a trip, the school play or sports day – checking whether students understand the key ideas and what they think of the author's writing.

- Will wants Year 10 to embrace positive behaviours. Having specified what he hopes students will do, he could ask students, "How could this help you in the future?"
- Janine needs students to stay at college for afternoon lessons. She could highlight the problems students may face if they don't attend, both distant (having to retake GCSEs a second time) and immediate (like phone calls home); or she could ask them what passing the retake would mean to them and their families.

Key idea

To show students a topic or an action matters, we can ask:

- **What problem does this address?**
- **How can I prompt students to see this is personally meaningful?**

We can further emphasise the value of an action through our framing of the effort required.

2.2 If students don't think it's worth the effort

Students must see the value of learning, as we've discussed, but they must also believe that it's worth the effort (and risk) required. Offered identical choices, people respond differently depending on how the costs and benefits are presented:[80] this section examines how best to present the consequences of students' choices.

1) We can encourage learning by minimising costs and highlighting benefits

People prefer immediate benefits and deferred costs (where "costs" include making an effort, or doing one thing when they'd rather do another). For example, when choosing what to watch that evening, people pick films like *Four Weddings and a Funeral*; they defer films like *Schindler's List* (which are good to have seen – a delayed benefit – but less immediately enjoyable) to a future evening.[81] Learning, however, incurs immediate costs (time and effort) for benefits which are deferred and hard to imagine (future understanding, satisfaction and success).[82] Even concrete benefits – like money – may not motivate students if they are deferred: offering students $20 for test performance, payable immediately, made them work harder, but offering $20, payable a month later, did not.[83]

> *People prefer immediate benefits and deferred costs; learning offers immediate costs for deferred benefits*

To make learning seem worth the effort, we must redress this balance, making benefits feel more immediate and costs more distant. Often, we describe future benefits – "This technique will help you next year" – but we can emphasise how soon they'll arise: "This technique will help with the next task." We could also try to make future benefits feel more vivid, asking students to "Imagine how satisfied you'll feel when you've mastered this." Conversely, we can downplay the size of a task – "Just complete these two questions" (then the next two), rather than "Complete this page" – and its difficulty: "It looks hard, but as soon as you've done the first question you'll see you can do it." Alternatively, we can reframe costs as benefits: independent work offers autonomy ("You don't need my help"); extra practice promotes mastery ("Complete these questions, and you'll crack this technique"); peer support is a chance for connection ("You'll face similar challenges, you can help each other solve many of them").[84] Perhaps most importantly, as soon as students begin, we can ensure they experience the benefits which justify their efforts, by using bite-size goals (discussed in Chapter 1) and pausing frequently to ensure students recognise their success (discussed in Chapter 5).

> *Show that the effort is worth it, by highlighting immediate benefits, while deferring, downplaying or reframing costs*

2) We can highlight potential losses to maintain effort and encourage risk-taking

People care more about (and work harder to avoid) losses, than they care about making equivalent gains.[85] For example, students given $20 (and risking losing it) tried harder on a test than students who could make $20.[86] We can encourage students to maintain past achievements by emphasising that they are in credit: "You got eight out of ten last week, revise tonight so your score doesn't dip." And we can put them in credit (rather than waiting for them to succeed), putting three ticks on the board at the start of the lesson (or a hundred merits at the start of term), and encouraging students not to lose them. (If it's realistic, we could do something similar with an individual's report, recording their successes at the start of the lesson, then challenging them not to lose their good report.) Keeping a student in credit may be particularly important if they have behaved poorly and are teetering between recovery and disaster: "This is only half done" (which is disappointing) may be more true than "This is already half done" (so keep going), but the less a student feels they have to lose, the more tempted they may be to give up entirely. (Reframing the time period may help: "You've nearly completed the unit" rather than "You've just started the lesson.") We can challenge poor behaviour and still keep students in credit: "Shouting out is unacceptable: you've done loads of good work this lesson, don't ruin things now." Putting students in credit should encourage them to maintain it.

> *Show students they are in credit: encourage them not to lose it*

Usually we prevent students from missing out, offering additional chances and help whenever they want it. This is generous, but it may devalue what we offer: if students can get help any time, they can always wait until tomorrow. People hate missing out, which is why advertisements and websites emphasise there are "Only a few left," and sales "Must end soon."[87] Students don't like missing out on learning either: told that university rules forbade hearing a speech advocating compulsory drug-testing, students were more interested in hearing it and more enthusiastic about drug testing.[88] We could mention what students might miss out on to elicit their interest: "This is fascinating, but we're short of time/they took it off the syllabus/it's not really appropriate for your year group, so we can't discuss it." If students object sufficiently, we can make a brief exception, "As long as you listen intently"; alternatively, this may tempt students to learn more themselves. This approach could make opportunities and resources seem more valuable too: "Today is your final chance to discuss last week's essay with me" (we can bend this rule later if necessary); "I only have twelve revision guides available today – who plans to use one tonight?" People are particularly swayed by appeals not to miss out (through inaction) when acting feels risky (speaking publicly, or getting feedback, for example):[89] it may be better to ask students to share work so as not to "miss out on feedback" rather than to "benefit from feedback."

> *Encourage students not to miss out on support, opportunities and learning*

Applications

- Helen's Year 6 class are "undismayed" by poor work. She might try to make the costs feel more immediate, by discussing pupils' confusion when they read or their struggle to articulate and understand ideas now, rather than what they need for SATs or secondary school. Or she might encourage them not to miss out on the chance to learn skills which may never be repeated.
- Will wants Year 10 to embrace positive behaviours. He might emphasise the benefits: "Understanding this now means everything will fall into place later in the lesson/you can leave the room feeling proud." Alternatively, he could reframe the costs as benefits: "We're emphasising independent, focused work this term because we want you to be able to work independently, without relying on us."
- Janine wants students to attend afternoon lessons, but the costs of attending are immediate; the benefits are delayed. She could highlight the immediate benefits of attending by ending each lesson with a review emphasising what students have just learned. She could also put students who are not attending in credit, highlighting their success in other subjects, and encouraging them not to let this slip.

> **Key idea**
>
> **How we frame the costs and benefits of learning influences how appealing it seems. We can decide what to emphasise by considering:**
>
> - **How can I decrease costs and emphasise benefits? (To encourage action)**
> - **How can I put students in credit? (To maintain progress)**
> - **How can I encourage students not to miss out?**

How people respond reflects not just what we emphasise, but what they prioritise – achieving success or avoiding failure:[90] we may wish to emphasise immediate benefits to one student, and the risk of missing out to another. The importance of immediate costs and benefits has implications for our use of sanctions, which we discuss in Chapter 6. Next, however, we turn to two powerful social motivations for change: role models and social norms.

2.3 If students don't aspire to learn

People are influenced by the actions of others: by individual role models – discussed in this section – and by the behaviour of the group, discussed below. A role model shows what's possible, giving people confidence and inspiration, a figure to emulate and to judge themselves against.[91] A personal story – describing a potential role model – has proved more effective at encouraging people to get vaccinated, and students to apply to university, than similar messages conveyed through impersonal texts.[92] Young people particularly seem to prefer guidance from peers, and non-experts who seem similar to them (rather than distant experts or official sources).[93] But while having a role model improves students' behaviour and academic engagement,[94] the influence role models have is not straightforward. It's often assumed that young people are heavily influenced by celebrities, but most students name parents and immediate family members as role models.[95] Moreover, people may have many role models: a role model can be positive or negative, admired for general or specific attributes, and can act as an immediate example or a distant hero.[96] For example, asked about their "role model," students named family members, but asked about their "reading role model," half named a teacher or librarian, and a third named a peer.[97] We cannot make students admire a role model: people choose who they look up to,[98] usually selecting role models who seem in some way similar (for example, of the same gender and ethnicity) and relevant (in particular, to their future plans).[99] However, we can introduce students to five types of potential role model, in person and through stories.

> *We may influence students by introducing them to a range of potential role models*

Teachers

Students learn from teachers' actions and their explanation of those actions. We convey what we accept and expect implicitly through our behaviour (how we focus on a task; how we listen to students) and our language (using "denominator" rather than "bottom number"; asking for "ideas" rather than "the answer"). Colleagues may help us to identify what we are conveying: I hadn't thought about the message my chaotic desk sent about organisation, until a friend mentioned it. Explaining our behaviour helps: students may miss what we're doing, or may not understand why we're doing it. We could highlight actions students might miss: how we have prepared for a lesson, and how the scheme of work reflects our understanding of the topic, for example. (This may be particularly important for social behaviour: "Do you notice I'm keeping my tone calm, and level – can you match this?") We can also clarify the thinking behind actions they do see: students' understanding improved when teachers began explaining what they were thinking as they read texts in class.[100] Modelling what we expect and explaining our choices is powerful, but it has limits: for example, we may need to do things we don't want students to do. (We can explain these discrepancies: "We don't interrupt each other – but I may break this rule if the discussion is going off-track.") More importantly, students may not want to emulate us: other role models may prove more persuasive.

The teacher as role model	Pros:	Cons:	Application:
	Constantly visible Expert in what students should do	Students may not want to emulate us or see us as relatable	Describe what you're doing, and why

Peers

Students' peers are obvious and immediate role models: a student's success shows peers they can succeed too.[101] To highlight a student as a role model, we can share what they have done – a good answer, for example – and how they have achieved it, asking them to explain their actions, or asking their peers: "Did anyone notice what made Ada's answer compelling?" If students believe their classmate's success is unattainable however – because it's down to talent, or it's too late for them to refine their work – they may be unmoved.[102] Moreover, within-class comparisons are problematic: students may dislike their peer, while those highlighted as role models may decrease their effort to avoid the limelight.[103] This makes slightly older students better potential role models: our students can still aspire to the role models' successes (there's still time to work harder), and older students are not under the same social pressure. For example, a talk from a recent graduate encouraged university applications,[104] and letters from current undergraduates to students with good GCSEs (in schools where few students attended top universities) increased applications and acceptances.[105] It's common to highlight past students' results and university or college places; we may also want them to describe what they did, and how it helped. If we can't get past students into the classroom, we can ask them to write or record a message, or we can describe their efforts and achievements ourselves. If their accomplishments seem within reach,[106] peers can be credible role models.

Highlight peers as role models	Pros:	Cons:	Application:
	Credible and accessible	Socially complicated; their success must look attainable	Share a student's work or a description of their actions

Distant heroes

Distant heroes can be powerful role models. Personal encounters are particularly influential: Michelle Obama visited Elizabeth Garett Anderson School in London, met the school's students in Oxford and invited a group to the White House; students' GCSE results jumped.[107] We can create personal encounters by inviting interesting local residents, or asking Speakers for Schools, which organises free talks from successful people. Stories can be influential too: one experiment asked students to read accounts of either the achievements or the struggles of Einstein, Marie Curie and Michael Faraday. Studying their achievements had little effect, but reading about their struggles – personal and scientific – led students to feel a connection with them, and gain higher grades; students with low prior attainment improved the most.[108] We can discuss the lives and struggles of characters, past or present, who exemplify the behaviours we hope students will adopt.

Highlight distant heroes as role models	Pros:	Cons:	Application:
	Inspirational	Hard to organise personal encounters	Share a story of a hero's life and struggles

Existing role models

We may be able to influence students through their existing role models (usually their parents).[109] Family members' actions convey a message about what's valuable: we can invite them to adopt desirable habits, like reading books together and playing number games. (There may be limits to what parents are able, or willing, to do: change is more likely if we ask them to adopt a single, simple habit, like reading together for fifteen minutes a day.) Alternatively (and more simply), we can ask families to emphasise and explain what they are doing already. This may mean making their actions more visible: reading for pleasure before children are in bed, rather than afterwards. Or it may mean explaining their actions: describing how they organise themselves for the working day, for example. We can reinforce this by asking students to describe how a role model exhibits the behaviours we are encouraging: "When does your role model have to persevere with a difficult task?"

Ask existing role models to act/explain their actions	Pros: Students already look up to them	Cons: Harder for teachers to know or influence their actions	Application: Ask family members to explain when they focus or persevere

Students themselves

Finally, we can help students see themselves as role models. When people try to persuade others to do something, they persuade themselves, and behave differently as a result.[110] For example, new undergraduates were asked to create a message to convince future students that their initial worries about university would dissipate: three years later, *the creators* felt happier, and got higher grades.[111] Such experiences lead students to see their role differently, as I discovered when I took my Year 9 students to teach a lesson in a primary school. Students whose behaviour sometimes disappointed rose to the occasion: one student I often struggled with noticed rude graffiti on a resource, and immediately spirited it away. We may motivate students by asking them to create a message to persuade others to study the subject, or to focus in lessons (reminding them of this message helps).[112] Indeed, asking Year 12 to write something to motivate Year 9 may help us to inspire both Year 12 *and* Year 9.

Help students see themselves as role models	Pros: A powerful way to take on a new identity	Cons: Relies on students taking the first step	Application: Ask students to persuade others to learn

Applications

- Helen's Year 6 class are "undismayed" by poor work: she could invite past pupils to tell her class how secondary school works and what they need to do to succeed. Or she might ask parents to emphasise what they do well and why it matters.
- Will wants Year 10 to embrace positive behaviours: he could ask students to read about historical or contemporary figures who demonstrate the behaviours he wants to promote; or he could ask them to write advice about how to succeed for future Year 10 students.
- Janine needs students to stay at college for afternoon lessons: she might invite students who passed their resits last year to speak to her current class.

> ## Key idea
>
> **Role models are powerful but complicated influences. We cannot make students look up to others, but we can highlight the actions and thoughts of potential role models. We may ask ourselves:**
>
> - **Who does this well (teachers, peers, distant heroes or existing role models)?**
> - **Who do students already look up to?**
> - **How can I help students see themselves as role models?**

The effect of an individual role model can be powerful; the effect of knowing what most other students are doing – the social norm – may be even more so.

2.4 If students don't accept it

Emphasising social norms – what others are doing – influences people's behaviour by clarifying what others may expect of them. One kind of norm is what the school and teachers expect: our rules and requests; "work hard, don't call out, help others." The other norm is what's prevalent: what students see their peers doing (whether or not this is what the school expects).[113] One study examined these norms by obscuring car windscreens with a flyer and seeing whether (unaware) participants dropped it as litter.[114] If the car park was clean, or if rubbish had been swept into piles (emphasising expected behaviour), people were unlikely to litter. However, if there was a lot of rubbish already (prevalent behaviour), participants were more likely to litter, particularly if they saw someone else do so. A study in the Netherlands (attaching flyers to bikes rather than cars) found similar results, and showed that breaches of one norm encouraged breaches of others: graffiti encouraged littering.[115] We can influence students by clarifying what we expect, highlighting what's prevalent (if it's positive) and shifting undesirable norms gradually.

1) We can clarify what's expected

We may assume students know our expectations: we explain them early in the year (and some seem obvious). But what looks like resistance is often "lack of clarity":[116] students forget, and face differing expectations between home and school, and between Maths and English.[117] They need "crystal-clear direction."[118] First, we can use concrete language to clarify, for example, whether "individual work" permits quiet discussion, whispered conversation, or no talking at all. Explaining what not to do often removes ambiguity: "I don't want you to ask your partner, even if you feel stuck" (practice helps too – it's discussed in Chapter 4). Even once we've explained, students are likely to need frequent, patient reminders until they form habits. This may mean using signs: at Mossley Hollins High School, every door has a sign at eye-level, stating, "Thank you for holding the door open. Your manners are appreciated." It may mean the environment we create: Cookery teacher Andrew Hartshorn runs his classroom like a professional kitchen; he rings a bell for attention, students respond to instructions with "Oui chef." It may simply be through our actions and body language: stepping out of the classroom to supervise transition between lessons; a moving finger to indicate that students should be writing. Every time students succeed or fail, we can reiterate our expectations: "What did Erin forget/do brilliantly just now?" (We can also revisit the importance of the expectation – using strategies discussed earlier in this chapter – and reinforce the message by sanctioning students who intentionally breach expectations; sanctions are discussed in Chapter 6.) The more consistent norms are – in our classroom, and across the school – and the more reminders we offer, the easier it is for students to follow them. Once students know what we expect, we can emphasise that it's also prevalent.

Keep clarifying exactly what you expect (and what you don't expect)

---

2) We can emphasise positive prevalent behaviour

A student's peers are their "primary audience."[119] People are influenced by what's expected, but they are influenced more by what their peers are doing:[120] students know they should be working, but if no one else is, they don't. Indeed, "when there is a clash between the peer culture and the teacher's management procedures, the peer culture wins every time."[121] We've discussed people's preference for immediate benefits (and dislike of immediate costs). Most students' goals are immediate:

> Not to become a successful adult but to be a successful child. The motivational bias towards gaining the approval of one's peer group probably reaches its peak in the teenage years. Children work out with unerring accuracy what kind of behaviours gain approval and what sort of approach to school will result in the maximum of admiration and respect.[122]

This means that peers influence students' academic achievement, the social groups they join,[123] and the choices they make, such as whether to ask for help applying to university.[124] This can be a barrier to learning, but it can also be an opportunity.

Students usually do what their peers do

Students measure themselves against their peers, so we can encourage them to learn by highlighting their peers' efforts. This is powerful because students may have an inaccurate impression of their classmates' behaviour: if everyone is downplaying how hard they are trying, for example, or how much revision they are doing. Telling doctors they were over-prescribing antibiotics, compared to their peers (correcting their impressions), made them prescribe less.[125] First, we must assess prevalent behaviour accurately. It's easy to feel that the classroom is chaotic because two or three students are unfocused, or that bafflement is widespread because a few students are confused. An objective measure of students' behaviour helps:

- How many students understood, according to our exit ticket?
- How many students are writing right now?
- How many students did their homework?

If the results are positive, we can share them with students in neutral terms: "I can see twenty-seven of you are writing already." We can also share good work (and describe how common it is), or display average number of students completing homework, or average time students have spent practising online. (Conveying averages is better than singling out individuals: they may decrease their effort to avoid further scrutiny.)[126] When we make a positive, prevalent norm more visible, we encourage other students to follow it.

> *Tell students what their peers are doing (if they're doing well)*

3) We can shift norms gradually

If most students aren't doing what we would hope however, highlighting it may make things worse. Often, people encourage change by emphasising that a problem is "regrettably frequent": this may be "true and well intentioned," but behind the message, "'Many people are doing this undesirable thing,' lurks the powerful and undercutting descriptive message 'Many people are doing this.'"[127] For example, telling people how much electricity they are using compared to their neighbours leads above-average users to use less – but below-average users use more.[128] So complaining that "You're being too noisy" may encourage noise; noting that "No one has yet drawn a pentagon correctly" may suggest that no one will; telling students they are averaging fifteen minutes' independent study a day may encourage those doing more to cut back. Nor can we lie about prevalent behaviour: claiming that everyone's working hard – if it's not true – simply diminishes our credibility.

> *If most students aren't doing what you want, don't emphasise it*

When undesirable behaviour is prevalent, people come to accept it: this creates a sticky norm, which is hard to shift.[129] People resist big changes in what's expected: banning alcohol (under Prohibition) was seen as illegitimate; otherwise law-abiding Americans embraced illegal drinking.[130] Similarly, if most teachers let students chat while working, a teacher who demands silence will face resistance from students (and may not get support from parents or leaders). To shift sticky norms, we must change expectations gradually, enforce each step, then emphasise progress. For example, while Prohibition failed, smoking has been restricted incrementally: a ban on workplace smoking made a ban on smoking in pubs (also work-places) hard to resist.[131] We can establish – and enforce – a new expectation which modestly improves the current situation: five minutes' silent writing, or a polite greeting at the door. (This builds on the idea of breaking change into smaller goals, discussed in Chapter 1.) When the new expectation becomes prevalent, we can introduce the next step: five minutes' writing becomes ten; a polite greeting becomes students going straight to their seats. Highlighting changing norms encourages people to go along with the new trend (telling people meat consumption is falling encourages them to order vegetarian food, for example):[132] we can emphasise what's changing, "I've had more contributions than ever before today . . ." or simply highlight progress; "Excellent start from Andy, Jen's writing already, well done Mohammed . . ." Stories about groups which have adopted new norms encourage listeners to do the same,[133] so we could reinforce our message by describing how other (perhaps older) students have changed. We can shift sticky norms by gradually introducing new expectations, enforcing them, and emphasising progress.

Introduce new expectations gradually, enforce them, and emphasise positive trends

---

Applications:

- Helen's Year 6 class are "undismayed" by poor work: she could highlight any improvement among her Year 6 pupils: noting that she saw the "best homework" she'd ever received yesterday, for example.
- Will wants Year 10 to embrace positive behaviours. He could clarify what he expects, then highlight the existing trend: students are working better than they ever have for him, and he wants them to keep improving.
- Janine needs students to stay at college for afternoon lessons. She is facing a sticky norm: she might begin to address this by ensuring all students are arriving on time in the morning, and are present at the end of lunch, and then tackle afternoon attendance.

Key idea

Norms are powerful, but hard to change. We can ask ourselves:

- **Do students know exactly what I want from them? When do they need reminders?**
- **Is prevalent behaviour positive? If so, how can I highlight this?**
- **Am I facing a sticky norm? If so, what new expectation would start to shift it?**

We can do much to encourage positive norms in our classrooms - but it's easier for students to follow norms (and for teachers to enforce them) if they are applied consistently around the school. (We discuss how leaders can encourage this kind of consistency in Chapter 7.)

Conclusion

No magical method motivates all students: what inspires one may leave another unmoved. But we can test these strategies easily - often simply by rephrasing requests: rather than "Please start," we can try reducing the immediate cost by saying "Please start the first question," for example. To demonstrate that learning is valuable, we can ask:

- How can I show students it matters?
- How can I show that it's worth the effort?

And to show that it's socially desirable, we can ask:

- What role models could inspire students?
- How can I show students that it's the norm?

It's easier to teach motivated students, but motivation is not a prerequisite for learning (as we discussed in the Introduction). It matters most in getting students started, but making the first steps easier may help here too (discussed in Chapter 4). Past success motivates continued effort, so we can increase students' motivation once they have begun (discussed in Chapter 5). Most importantly, wanting to act doesn't guarantee students will act - they may forget, or prioritise something else. The next chapter looks at turning their good intentions into commitments, and plans.

✓ Checklist

I have specified what I want students to do (based on Chapter 1).	
I inspire and motivate students to do it	
1) If students don't see the value in learning, I . . .	
• Emphasise the problem – helping students feel the need for the action	*Asking students to tackle a sum which they don't yet have the maths to solve.*
• Make it personal – help students see its value to them	*"How could what we're learning in this unit be valuable to you?"*
2) If students don't think it's worth the effort, instead of telling them it will be worth it in the future, I . . .	
• Highlight immediate benefits; minimise costs	*"I'd just like you to do the first question, which will show you how useful this approach is."*
• Encourage students to avoid losses	*"You're doing well, don't let things slip"/"Don't miss out on this opportunity"*
3) If students don't aspire to it, I . . .	
• Show what I do	*"As I'm reading this text, I'm asking myself, 'Why is the author telling me this?'"*
• Show that peers are succeeding	*"One of my students last year struggled with this, but she overcame this, by . . ."*
• Show how great figures succeed	*Mathematician Maryam Mirzakhani questioned her teachers relentlessly when she was unsure (in her second language).*
• Show existing role models' successes	*Asking parents to emphasise how hard they work, and why.*
• Let students persuade themselves	*Asking students to write advice for next year's class about how to learn effectively.*
4) If students don't accept it, I . . .	
• Ensure students know what they should do	*Stating exactly what students should (and shouldn't) do when they enter the room.*
• Emphasise how many students are already doing things right	*"Almost everyone has started writing already . . ."*
• Shift norms gradually: raise expectations and highlight progress	*Describing how many students are now doing what I hoped they would do*
Next, I help students **plan** (Chapter 3), **initiate** (Chapter 4) and **follow up** (Chapter 5) change.	

Copyright material from Harry Fletcher-Wood (2022), *Habits of Success: Getting Every Student Learning*, Routledge

Workshop 2: helping students see why the topic matters

What's the situation?

Rachel's students don't care about the things she most wants them to care about. Rachel recently took responsibility for the Personal, Social and Health Education curriculum in her school. She's excited to teach her students to stay safe and to thrive, but she has two big concerns. First, the subject isn't valued: most students are sceptical about what school can teach them about life, and older students are increasingly cynical. Second, what students learn in the classroom doesn't seem to influence their actions: students know smoking is dangerous, for example, but some are still tempted to try it. (This situation reflects both the limited interest most teachers encounter - whatever their subject - from some students; and the barriers which anyone in a pastoral role faces in helping students to behave safely.)

What would you suggest?

1) What is the fundamental challenge? What habit or steps would solve it?
2) How would you inspire students to act?
3) Do students need to commit to action?
4) How can you make it easy?
5) How can you help students keep going?

Step 1) Specify the change

Rachel realises that the curriculum suffers from vague aims. The big goals include teaching safe behaviour, good citizenship and global awareness, but the contribution of individual lessons to these goals is not always clear. Rachel encapsulates the purpose of each unit in a single scenario, and the behaviour she hopes students will adopt if they face it, for example, if they are:

- Offered drugs or cigarettes, they refuse.
- Concerned about a peer's health, they tell a trusted adult.
- In a dangerous situation, they leave it.

This allows Rachel to design each lesson to provide students with either the knowledge, insight, experience or practice they need to meet the scenario.

Step 2) Inspire and motivate students

Rachel wants to convince students that what they are learning matters. Many students see these lessons as irrelevant, or as less important than academic subjects; the students who most need guidance seem least inclined to accept it from their teachers. Clear goals for each lesson and unit help; Rachel also tries to:

Show it matters

Rachel tries to demonstrate that each unit focuses on genuine problems faced by students like them. She has tried offering the rationale - telling students the prevalence of specific risks, such as hospitalisation after excessive drinking – but she knows they feel remote: "It'll never happen to me." So Rachel begins each unit by telling a true story in which a student faces a dilemma or challenge, like a problematic relationship or peer pressure to smoke. Highlighting the decisions they face makes the situations more compelling and engenders students' curiosity: they only discover each individual's response, and the consequences, at the end of the unit, once they know more about the topic.

Make it immediately worthwhile

Students often ignore pastoral guidance because they worry more about immediate consequences (like their friends' approval) and less about distant ones (like their future health). Rachel shows that lessons are immediately worthwhile by concluding each with a question: "What do you know now, and how could it prove useful?" She offers immediate justifications for the decisions she hopes students will make too, highlighting immediate costs (smoking makes you less fit straight away) and downplaying apparent benefits (peers' disapproval may prove fleeting). She also reframes potential costs as benefits ("Resisting peer pressure means you're making your own choices") and opportunities ("You're not just refusing a cigarette, you're choosing to get fit").

Highlight role models

Rachel wants to provide students with convincing, relatable role models. She:

- Uses the individuals whose stories introduce each unit as role models in subsequent units: "Think about how Khadija responded when she was under pressure in the last unit – what do you think she would do in this situation?"
- Describes the behaviour of heroic figures: asking students to show the determination and persistence of Civil Rights protesters, for example.
- Encourages students to see themselves as role models: she asks them to write advice to younger students at the end of each unit; she will use what they write in future years, but she hopes that offering advice will influence students' intentions too.

Emphasise social norms

Rachel worries that social norms – and students' inaccurate perceptions of what's prevalent – may lead them astray. For example, she knows her students overestimate how many of their peers are trying risky behaviour. She shares statistics – "Nationally, 87% of students don't touch drugs" – and emphasises changing trends: "Fewer and fewer under-sixteens have ever drunk alcohol." She hopes this will convince students that safe choices are also socially acceptable.

Step 3) Plan change

Rachel helps students make a plan, preparing them to act on their good intentions. Near the end of each unit, they are offered scenarios ("A friend asks you to look after a package for them for a few days, and not to open it," for example) and asked to plan what they would say and do in response.

Step 4) Initiate action

Rachel uses practice activities to prepare students to act on their plans (and to increase their confidence to do so). Students practise the scenarios they have planned, testing and refining their responses. They observe small-group role plays, pausing their actions and "rewinding," to explore individuals' choices, and the consequences of their words and actions.

Step 5) Follow up

Rachel does everything she can to track students' responses. She has a confidential post box outside her office, in which students can post questions and describe situations they have experienced. Each term, students complete an anonymous survey: Rachel asks about situations they have encountered, and their confidence in handling them. She feeds positive trends back to students – "most of you said you were confident to challenge a peer who was behaving inappropriately" – and uses their responses to create new scenarios and make units more realistic and relevant. Rachel offers feedback intended to help students feel resilient, independent and reflective – "The way Michael responded to that scenario exemplifies the calm confidence we hope you'll show" – and to highlight the school as a supportive community: "I'm really glad that so many of you are happy to tell your peers when you're struggling."

Conclusion

Rachel knows her influence is limited, but she hopes to affect students' actions by clarifying what they should do, emphasising why it matters, and preparing them to act. She may not persuade every student, but she hopes they will at least recognise the choices they have, and approach them more thoughtfully.

3 How can we help students to commit to action?

Specify the change: pick a priority, then choose a powerful habit or small step to achieve it

Inspire and motivate students to value the change

PLan change: ask students to commit to action

Initiate action: make starting easy

Follow up: help students keep going

Chapter map: how can we help students to commit to action?

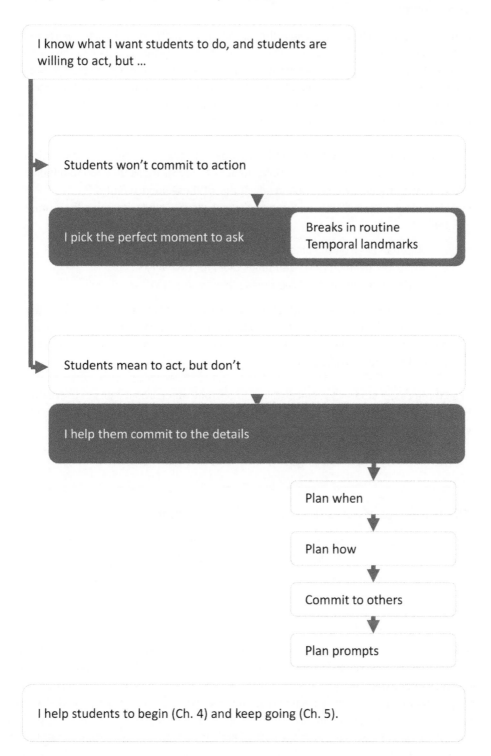

I know what I want students to do, and students are willing to act, but ...

Students won't commit to action

I pick the perfect moment to ask

Breaks in routine
Temporal landmarks

Students mean to act, but don't

I help them commit to the details

Plan when

Plan how

Commit to others

Plan prompts

I help students to begin (Ch. 4) and keep going (Ch. 5).

Copyright material from Harry Fletcher-Wood (2022), *Habits of Success: Getting Every Student Learning*, Routledge

The problem

In the 1990s, carefully designed advertising campaigns more than doubled awareness of the importance of eating five portions of fruit and vegetables a day. In the same period, the proportion of people actually eating five a day did not change.[134] People can be aware, inclined and even motivated to act, but still delay, forget or get diverted. We may specify what students should do (based on Chapter 1), motivate them to do it (using Chapter 2), then find they still don't do it. For example:

- Ollie Lovell had carefully refined his approach to teaching crucial mathematical concepts, to offer students multiple chances to revisit those they found difficult. However, students weren't taking advantage of these opportunities.[135]
- Helen took responsibility for three pupils who were behind in learning their times tables:

    o   Alex had been on the nine-times table for two weeks.
    o   Brian had been on the seven-times table for two weeks.
    o   Carla had been on the three-times table for *five months*.

- Samira provided students with extensive revision resources, but they didn't use them: she got emails "asking if I can help them with X when X is already provided on the website I've already told them all about . . . parents want to help but often do not know how to help either."

In all three cases, students seemed willing to act, but weren't doing so. In our frustration, we may resort to nagging and sanctions – but there may be better ways to help students act on their good intentions.

The principle: ask students to commit to a plan

We can encourage students to commit to action by timing our request perfectly; we can make action more likely by helping them plan the details.

3.1 If students won't commit to action

We usually ask students to act when we want them to do something – but if we ask in advance, they're more likely to agree to it. For example, one study asked workers to increase their pension contributions immediately: most refused. Refusers were then asked to increase their contributions when they next got a pay rise (in three months' time): most agreed.[136] Partly, this is because people prefer immediate benefits and deferred costs (as we discussed in Chapter 2): asking in advance defers the costs. Partly, it's because people believe their future self will be better than their present self (some smokers were so sure of this that they were willing to bet on it: they saved money, only getting it back if they had quit smoking a year later).[137] It's also a question of confidence: students are more confident about a test a few weeks beforehand than on the day itself.[138] So when we ask students in advance, costs feel distant, and they are optimistic they'll be doing better by the time they have to act. (Students willingly impose essay deadlines on themselves at the start of term, complete with penalties for missing them.)[139] If we want students to act, we should ask them to commit to it before they need to begin: "Tell me how you'll focus better next lesson/week/term."

> *Ask students to commit to action in advance*

Temporal landmarks – breaks in routine, or meaningful moments – are another opportunity for students to commit to change. They have two important effects: first, they disrupt existing habits; when people move home, for example, they have to find a new way to get to work; they can be tempted to begin walking and cycling.[140] Second, they promote reflection about what people really want (and allow them to leave past failures behind). For example, people are more likely to go to the gym, and to search for a new diet, after personal landmarks (their birthday) and collective ones (the new year, public holidays, even Mondays).[141] Opportunities abound in school: both obvious landmarks (the new term; changing class or school), and unwanted frustrations (like unexpected room changes). Obvious as they may seem however, we sometimes miss them, because they are disruptive for us too: dealing with the room change; getting back into routine after a holiday; working out where to seat a new student. We can use these landmarks to ask students to commit to specific changes: "The new topic (term/class/school) is a fresh start: what will you do to work more effectively?" Alternatively, we can promote broader reflection, asking students what they are proud of, and what they most want to change. (If we need students to commit to change and lack an obvious landmark, we can create one:[142] fifth play, tenth book, twentieth lesson, hundredth quiz.) Influencing students' self-perceptions and efforts at these landmarks can initiate a virtuous cycle with a lasting impact: their progress convinces them they can succeed, promoting greater effort.[143]

> *Ask students to make commitments at temporal landmarks*

Applications

- Ollie's students weren't reviewing key ideas: he could use his next test as a landmark to highlight topics on which they're struggling, asking students to commit to addressing them.
- Helen's pupils have been stuck on specific times tables for weeks: she's new to working with them, which offers a fresh start; she can ask them to commit to more effective learning habits.
- Samira's students aren't using revision resources: she could ask them to make fresh commitments before the next half-term or holiday.

> ## Key idea
>
> **Schools are built around temporal landmarks, but the pressure we are under, espe-
> cially at the start and end of term, means we don't always capitalise on them.
> We can help students commit to change by selecting promising moments to ask
> them. We can consider:**
>
> - **When do students have to begin? Can I ask them beforehand?**
> - **What landmarks could I use (personal, collective, or created)?**

We can use these moments to convince students that action is a good idea (using Chapter 2) and ask them to commit to action. To ensure they make good on their commitment however, we need to help them plan when and how to act; we address this next.

3.2 If students mean to act, but don't

People often mean to act, but don't: they delay and forget; they face obstacles and tempting alternatives.[144] Making a detailed plan helps them overcome these barriers. For example, people invited for a flu vaccination were more likely to attend if their letter also encouraged them to plan a time to go (and to write it on the letter).[145] Planning particularly helps when people intend to act, their opportunities to do so are limited, and they struggle with self-control.[146] One particularly powerful approach evokes commitment – by inviting people to imagine their success and to identify an obstacle – then asks them to plan to overcome the obstacle. Primary school pupils taught this approach (for goals of their choice) attended more, behaved better, and gained higher grades.[147] This section examines four elements of effective planning: deciding when and how to act, committing to others, and preparing prompts.

> *Planning helps to turn good intentions into action*

1) Plan when

Students are more likely to act if they plan precisely when to do so. Usually however, we ask them to revise, or complete homework, but leave them to decide when to do it. Instead, we can ask them to record the task and to pick a time for it. We can help them choose times which are more likely to prompt action; times which are:

- Specific:[148] "First thing on Sunday," is better than "over the weekend."
- Distinct events:[149] "After football" is better than "5pm."
- Existing habits:[150] "After dinner every day" is a reliable cue, because students will almost certainly have dinner.

We can also help them choose times which suit different kinds of task. During the day, most people's energy and attentiveness peaks in the morning, dips towards lunchtime, then partially recovers in the evening (a quarter of people peak in the evening instead);[151] across the week, students work hardest on Mondays, then less each following day.[152] So if students are planning weekend or holiday study, we can encourage them to do detailed, analytical tasks earlier in the day (and week), to stop for lunch, and to complete more creative tasks later on.[153] Recording these plans allows students (parents, and us) to monitor their progress (and adapt their schedule accordingly). Planning when to act applies most obviously to independent tasks, but we could use it to help students plan change in lessons too: "I'll stop talking as soon as the teacher asks for my attention," or "I'll check my working after I finish the last question." Once students have chosen when to act, we can help them plan how to act.

> *Ask students to specify a good time to act*

2) Plan how

When a student has struggled, we often try to identify the obstacles and omissions which derailed them: "You intended to do it, what went wrong?" Planning the details in advance however - what to do, where and how - helps people achieve their goals (and anticipate barriers).[154] These plans are often framed as "If - then" statements: "If my brother gets home early, then I'll ask him to let me finish my homework before playing." Obvious as such responses may seem, planning them dramatically increases the chances that people act on their intentions.[155] We could anticipate barriers and suggest responses for students, as science teacher Jess Dumbreck has done; she displays an "If - then" sheet outside her classroom to overcome barriers to completing homework. It includes:

Lost my **Show My Homework** login details	1. Speak to tutor 2. Speak to head of year
Lost the homework pack	1. Check whether it has been uploaded to SMHW 2. Message Miss Dumbreck on SMHW 3. See whether you can use a friend's and complete the work on a separate piece of paper
Don't know if you have homework	1. You probably do - check SMHW 2. Ask a classmate

Alternatively, we could ask students to make these plans themselves. This may help them to regulate their behaviour in the classroom - "If you're frustrated, what will you do?" - and to work more independently: "If you get stuck, what should you do first?" Such plans particularly help when people are under pressure (and therefore forgetful):[156] we could prepare students for exams by asking them to consider questions such as, "If you can't answer the first question, what will you do instead?" Detailed plans prepare students for action: we can reinforce these plans by asking students to articulate their commitments.

> *Help students plan exactly what they need to do*

3) Commit to others

People are more likely to act if they tell others their plan. A private commitment seems insufficient: when people bet they will lose weight (a private commitment promising financial reward) fewer than one in five win.[157] Public commitments work better: displaying people's weight-loss goals in their gym increased their motivation, and how much weight they lost.[158] Likewise, when people tell friends or relatives their plan, they put themselves under pressure to act.[159] The effect of a public commitment will depend on classroom culture: students offered help applying to university were more likely to accept it among high-performing peers, but less likely to do so among low-performing peers.[160] (The students affected most were those who cared most what their peers thought of them.)[161] In a supportive classroom, we could ask students to commit to their peers, or display their goal (and plan) on the wall; alternatively, we could ask them to write their plan, and share it with their form tutor or a family member. Committing to others encourages students to act on their plans; prompts may remind them to act when the moment comes.

> *Ask students to share their plan with classmates, or supportive adults*

4) Prepare prompts

Prompts encourage students to act on their commitments – but they must be designed carefully. For example, drivers were more likely to wear a seatbelt if they were reminded just before getting into their car, but being reminded five minutes before getting in made no difference.[162] Effective prompts include deadlines, reminders, checklists and supporters.

Deadlines

Deadlines demand action. This is as true for adults as it is for students: when the National Science Foundation abolished deadlines for research proposals (allowing submission at any time instead), submissions halved.[163] As we discussed above, people are more likely to agree to act if we ask in advance ("I'll focus better next term"). But they won't start while the need to do so feels distant ("I can wait until next term");[164] and they usually only start working hard when they realise how much is left to do (around halfway through the time they have).[165] We can prompt students to start with an interim deadline: a quiz next week demands revision; an exam next year does not. To make a deadline feel pressing, we can place it in the "present" week or month: telling students they have "one week" may prompt action better than telling them they have "until next Thursday" (also a week, but not demanding action until next week).[166] Deadlines prompt students to begin sooner – from starting writing (to meet a deadline of finishing the first sentence within two minutes) to starting a project (to meet a deadline of producing a plan this month).

> *Deadlines get students started sooner*

Deadlines must be set carefully, however. Some researchers criticise them as controlling and demotivating, and suggest that students should set their own.[167] However, students who did set their own deadlines placed them too close together, then struggled to meet them.[168] We could frame deadlines as putting students in control: "I'm setting these deadlines to help you stay on top of your work"; or offer structured choices: "You can choose any date in the week before half-term." Deadlines can backfire: one experiment promised students cash to study, but students with weekly deadlines did less work than those with one big deadline after five weeks.[169] In this study however, if students missed a single weekly deadline, they forfeited any chance of reward: this implies we should monitor students' responses, changing our approach if they give up, or submit poor work just to meet a deadline.

Help students see the value of the deadline

Reminders

Reminders are another way to prompt students to act. In the classroom, we can remind students of their plans - "What did you decide to write first?" - and commitments: "What did you agree to do differently this lesson?" If students will be working outside the classroom, we can suggest they set their own reminders: an alarm for their homework, for example, or a note to themselves about how to use feedback. (Alternatively, we could ask them to identify an existing habit which will serve as a reminder: "What do you do every evening which could prompt you to remember your homework?") We could also send reminders ourselves (text messages successfully prompted students to complete university enrolment tasks, for example):[170] we could email the class reminders of key actions and deadlines.

Set reminders - or ask students to set their own

Checklists

If students need to remember several things, we can develop checklists. These are used to get the details right in many professions: to coordinate building projects, reduce medical errors, and help pilots respond safely under pressure.[171] They encourage action: a checklist (to help complete the form) increased applications for tax-free childcare more than a message emphasising the benefits.[172] A checklist can remind students of the steps needed to complete procedures, like drawing graphs or balancing equations correctly (I shared many examples in a previous book, *Ticked Off*).[173] We could help students create their own checklists too: everything they should bring to school each day, for example. The items on the checklist are a reminder, and the presence of a checklist is itself a reminder: we could put a presentation checklist on the cover of students' books, or a checklist for setting up lab equipment on students' desks. Checklists help students recall a series of actions.

Develop checklists to remind students of multiple tasks

Supporters

Peers and family members can remind and support students to act (building on students' commitments to them). Families usually want to help, but – without information from us – they aren't always clear what's expected, or how well their child is doing. Providing this information – about students' attendance, for example – helps parents prompt students to act.[174] Several projects have tested the effect of weekly text messages providing information (about upcoming tests and missing homework, for example) and prompts to discuss recent learning: these messages have increased attendance and exam grades.[175] We can ensure students get encouragement and practical support by keeping parents informed of our expectations, students' plans, and ways they can help: "Jamila has promised to revise her spellings for ten minutes on the way home, please ask her to tell you the words she has learned."

> Keep supporters informed, so they can help students to act

Applications

- Ollie's students weren't taking advantage of revision opportunities: he began getting them to specify exactly when and where they would act, and to set reminders; students seemed to do more homework as a result.[176]
- Helen took responsibility for three pupils who were behind in learning their times tables: she gave her pupils a target (learn the times table they were on by the end of term, two weeks away), and asked them to specify how they would practise (online games, flash cards, practice sheets) and when. Students picked a precise time after school and specified who would help at home. Their choices were stuck into their Reading Record books with a note to parents, making them accountable because the student had named them as helping. Three days later the class teacher tested all students: Brian and Carla passed while Alex missed by only two answers, two weeks ahead of target.
- Samira provided students with extensive revision resources, but they didn't use them: she could ask students to specify what they will revise; and provide a reminder by setting up an email auto-reply with a checklist of revision activities. She could share students' plans, and her guidance, with parents.

Key idea

Students may not act, even when they intend to. Planning the details makes action more likely. We can ask students:

- **When – exactly – will be a good moment to act?**
- **What barriers might you face? How can you overcome them?**
- **Who will you tell about your plan?**
- **What will prompt you to act: a deadline, a reminder or a supporter?**

Conclusion

We can help students act on their good intentions by considering:

* When is the best moment to ask students to commit?
* What plans will help them to act?

This kind of planning can make a big difference for one-off tasks – but making plans has short-lived effects, particularly for goals which require ongoing effort.[177] If we want students to act – and keep going – we need to make initiating action easy for them (Chapter 4) and help them turn isolated success into a habit (Chapter 5).

Checklist

I have **s**pecified what I want students to do (based on Chapter 1).
I have **i**nspired and **m**otivated students to do it (based on Chapter 2).

I help them commit to a **pl**an

1)   If students won't commit to action, I pick . . .

• A break in routine	*Asking students to make fresh commitments when they move classes.*
• A landmark: personal (a birthday), collective (the new year) or created (students' tenth essay)	*Asking students what they are proud of so far, and what they would like to be different in future.*

2)   If students meant to act, but don't, instead of leaving them to make plans themselves, **I ask them to . . .**

• Plan when they will act: a specific, distinct trigger for action, at a conducive time	*"I'll start revising immediately after breakfast."*
• Plan how they will act – where, how, and what barriers they may face	*"I'll study alone at my desk: if I'm invited to go out and see friends, I'll wait until I've finished."*
• Commit to others – share the plan with family, teachers or the class	*"Please text your parents what you plan to do and when, and ask them to remind you."*
• Prepare prompts: deadlines, reminders, checklists and supporters	*Asking students to set a reminder on their phone; give them a checklist to tick off when it goes off.*

Next, I help students to **i**nitiate (Chapter 4) and **f**ollow up (Chapter 5) change.

Copyright material from Harry Fletcher-Wood (2022), *Habits of Success: Getting Every Student Learning*, Routledge

Workshop 3: getting students to study independently

What's the situation?

Lucia's students respond well in lessons and seem enthusiastic about the subject and her teaching. However, when she sends them home to revise, practise or complete homework, they rarely do. Some students would rather not be studying, but most promise sincerely to complete the task, then return with vague reasons why they didn't. Lucia knows they face both personal barriers (like forgetfulness and disorganisation) and competing priorities (sports practice, other homework tasks, seeing friends). She has considered using lesson time for revision tasks, but she worries this will prevent her from covering the syllabus and will prepare students poorly for future independent study. (This situation came from a secondary school teacher – but I suspect we've all encountered something similar.)

What would you suggest?

1)   What is the fundamental challenge? What habit or steps would solve it?
2)   How would you inspire students to act?
3)   Do students need to commit to action?
4)   How can you make it easy?
5)   How can you help students keep going?

Step 1) Specify the change

Lucia's goal is clear: she wants students to complete homework and independent study tasks routinely (and well), without having to chase them. She reviews each independent task to ensure it's clear, and defines revision tasks precisely, for example, "Use your flashcards to test yourself on the definition of these ten terms until you can get each one right."

Step 2) Inspire and motivate students

Lucia doesn't think that motivation is the problem: students mean to act, but struggle to do so. Nonetheless, when she sets independent tasks, she emphasises:

*   The problems being disorganised will cause students in future study and work – and the opportunity she is offering for independence and responsibility.
*   Immediate benefits (she asks students to explain how recent homework tasks have helped them understand lessons better) and the risk of missing out.
*   School norms around homework completion, and the class's progress towards them: "Last week, all my Year 12s handed in their homework on time; this week more of you than ever handed in your homework on time too."

Step 3) Plan change

Students are often vague about when they will act: a plan to revise "over the weekend" is easily derailed by more tempting alternatives. Lucia wants to help students plan their time better. At the start of the new term, she shares a homework timetable, then asks students to:

Plan when: Lucia asks students to choose a specific event which will act as a cue, such as a meal.

Plan how: students identify where they will work, and consider potential problems (such as distractions from friends and siblings), and solutions (leaving their phone in another room, for example).

Commit to others: Lucia asks students to share their plan with a buddy and with their parents; the buddy is meant to text a reminder on the day they plan to do it; Lucia asks parents to check students have done it.

Plan prompts: Lucia sets deadlines which encourage action: she never gives students more than a week, as this seems to make prioritising the task harder, and forgetting the details easier. She makes the deadline meaningful (and the homework immediately useful) by setting a quiz about it on the day she collects it. And she changes the deadline from Wednesday to Thursday: this allows her to remind students about it the day before it's due in.

Step 4) Initiate action

Lucia makes checking what to do easy: she puts the task online, and puts a copy on a "homework wall" outside her classroom. She ensures students know how to begin – and feel confident – by explaining the task in class, and giving students time to complete the first step together. Finally, she ensures that the first independent step is familiar, and that trickier steps come later.

Step 5) Follow up

Lucia helps students create a homework habit. She sets and collects the homework on the same day each week, and encourages students to pick a regular time to complete it. She makes the task consistent, asking students to do the same two things (a revision task and an essay question) and presenting it in the same way (on an A4 sheet with a consistent structure). Lucia records students' homework submission on a wallchart, making it easier for students, and parents, to see what they have done – and, if students miss the deadline, she sets a time by which they must bring it to her, or complete it with her.

Conclusion

Lucia finds that her approach removes almost all barriers to students completing their homework. Initially, it takes her more time, but, once the new routine is established, she saves time and energy previously spent chasing them. Perhaps more importantly, when she needs students to revise for exams, it's easy to build on their existing good habits.

4 How can we encourage students to start?

Specify the change: pick a priority, then choose a powerful habit or small step to achieve it

Inspire and motivate students to value the change

PLan change: ask students to commit to action

Initiate action: make starting easy

Follow up: help students keep going

Chapter map: how can we encourage students to start?

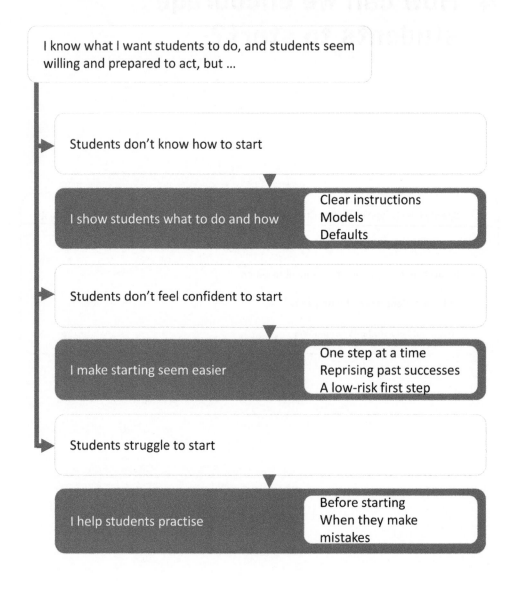

I know what I want students to do, and students seem willing and prepared to act, but …

Students don't know how to start

I show students what to do and how | Clear instructions
Models
Defaults

Students don't feel confident to start

I make starting seem easier | One step at a time
Reprising past successes
A low-risk first step

Students struggle to start

I help students practise | Before starting
When they make mistakes

I help students to keep going (Ch. 5).

Copyright material from Harry Fletcher-Wood (2022), *Habits of Success: Getting Every Student Learning*, Routledge

The problem

The first step is often the hardest one for students to take:

- Sam described "The class that won't work. When kids won't engage in correctly pitched work that they can do. They won't accept the smallest level of challenge."
- Samira provided students with extensive revision resources, but they didn't use them. (We discussed this problem in the previous chapter, but while planning to act should help, students may struggle to get started too.)
- Andy's trainees face "groups of students who are reluctant to take books out of bags and write anything. In Year 7 it might be just one student but as you go through the years more and more exhibit this behaviour."

Even if we have convinced students that an action is worthwhile (Chapter 2) and they have committed to acting at a specific time and place (Chapter 3), they may reach the cusp of action, but never begin. So, having examined ways to prepare students for action in Chapter 3, this chapter looks at shaping the moment itself, to overcome three barriers: students not knowing how to begin, not being confident to begin, or struggling to start effectively. At this point, the natural thing to do is to offer encouragement and add a little pressure. This can help, but there may be other ways to get them started.

The principle: make starting easy

We can help students to start by making action easier.

Making the first step easier has powerful effects. It can make starting more attractive: emphasising that signing up for literacy classes was easy tempted more parents to sign up than emphasising the benefits for their children.[178] It can boost students' confidence, improving their performance: students do better (and worry less) on tests with easier initial questions.[179] And it creates a sense of momentum: people who feel they have begun are more likely to keep going; customers given a car wash loyalty card with ten spaces (two of which had already been stamped) were more likely to complete it than customers given a card with eight spaces, none of which had been stamped.[180] Even when the task seems perfectly pitched, there is usually one more barrier we can remove, by clarifying where to start, making the first step seem easier, and practising.

4.1 If students don't know how to start

We can show and tell students what to do

Having chosen a habit for students to pursue (or a bitesize goal), we need to convey exactly what they need to do. Our instructions should be specific, concrete, sequential and observable.[181] Rather than asking students to "Focus completely on the task," we can specify: "Spend the entire time writing: first write every point you can think of, then review what you've written and add evidence." (Later, we can help students recognise the principles underlying their actions: "If you kept writing throughout, you focused well.") We should use as few words as possible to focus students on the most important points:[182] we could cut an instruction like "First identify exactly what it is that's most important in that paragraph, and then, once you've done that . . ." to "Identify the key point in the paragraph." None of this is surprising – communicating clearly is central to teaching – but it's not easy either. If students seem unclear how to start, it's worth asking them to describe the task. If they struggle, we can simplify (and, to improve our instructions in future, script key points in advance, and review them with a colleague). We can reinforce these instructions with demonstrations.

> *Check students know what to do: help them by being specific and succinct*

It's easier for students to do things they have seen done. They learn better if they are offered worked examples (step-by-step demonstrations of the task) and completion problems (partial models for them to complete – we return to completion problems below).[183] For academic tasks, we can offer model answers, then ask students to apply what we have demonstrated: for example, having shown students how to evaluate $\frac{1}{2} + \frac{1}{3}$ we can ask them to evaluate $\frac{1}{3} + \frac{1}{4}$.[184] We can make beginning even easier by showing students exactly how to start their answer: for example, giving students a sentence stem rather than a question; "Macbeth is ambitious, but he decides to 'proceed no further' in murdering Duncan because . . ." Worked examples help people learn social behaviour too:[185] we can show students how to cooperate effectively, or how to apologise to a peer, giving them an opening line: "So you'll begin your apology by saying 'I'm sorry I did that and . . .'" Like clear instructions, models are integral to teaching – but often (particularly in secondary schools) we underuse them, hoping to encourage independence and creativity: if students don't know how to start, show them.

> *Show students what to do*

We can set defaults

Defaults help people start more complicated tasks. Clear instructions contribute, but as students become more independent (and face harder tasks), increasingly they must decide how to begin: how to start an answer, what to revise first, when to contribute to a discussion. Defaults address two barriers to starting: choosing poorly, and getting stuck choosing. Pension enrolment illustrates these barriers well: historically, most teachers have enrolled (it's the default), but many younger private sector workers did not; they had to decide to enrol, choose a pension provider and complete the paperwork. Concerned about this, the government made pension enrolment the default: workers remained free to opt out, but the proportion enrolling in their twenties jumped, from 16% to over 60%.[186] The influence of defaults on behaviour has been demonstrated for many decisions, from signing up to green electricity tariffs (94% of customers stuck with a green tariff when it became the default, even though there was a cheaper alternative),[187] to registering for organ donation (98% of people are registered in countries where it's the default; 15% are registered in countries where people must sign up).[188] Defaults are powerful – and they're never neutral. By default, I graded students' work: they focused on the grade, and ignored my comments. I changed the default: I stopped writing grades on their work; students who wanted them had to return after the lesson and explain how they could improve (using my comments). (This reassured me they understood the feedback, demonstrated they really wanted the grade, and reassured them that they could improve on it.) A changed default encouraged students to engage with feedback. Defaults don't compel – people can always improve on them – but they are a powerful way to encourage action.

Defaults overcome barriers to beginning

Whenever students find it hard to begin (or to begin well), it's worth reviewing the defaults – theirs and ours. For example, if we want students to start checking their work more carefully, the current default (we correct any student errors) may not be helping. We could set a new default for students ("Always review your work against the checklist before submitting it") and for ourselves (return work if it contains errors we know students can fix). We can create defaults which apply in every lesson ("If you get stuck, go back to the model") and for specific tasks ("For questions like this, a good structure/first step/opening line is . . ."). Our defaults can encourage focus ("No talking for the first five minutes writing"), perseverance ("I'll always ask what you've tried before helping you") and contribution ("No one gets to speak again until everyone has spoken once"). A default need not be perfect: it just needs to be good enough to get students started.

Set defaults which get students started

Caveat: as students succeed, reduce guidance and encourage choice

Initially, clear guidance about how to start is essential. The better students are doing, however, the less we should offer. Novices need guidance, but as they gain expertise, it comes to distract them:[189] once students know what to do, we can reduce our guidance (reintroducing it if they struggle). Defaults get students going, but don't teach deciding how to start. We can practise these decisions ("Write an opening sentence for each of these five essay titles") and encourage thoughtful deviation from the default ("I suggest starting with Question 2, but you're welcome to do this another way if you can tell me why"). People are more enthusiastic about their choices than they are about defaults. Perhaps surprisingly however, offering a choice while stressing our recommendation seems to elicit commitment while encouraging the desired choice: rather than "Will you come to the revision class?" (no default) or "I expect everyone to come" (a default which does not engender commitment), we could ask students "Will you give yourself the best chance of success by coming to the revision class?"[190] Clear guidance and defaults help students begin: gradually removing them teaches students to begin independently.

Reduce guidance to help students choose how to begin

Applications

- Sam described trying to influence "The class that won't work." Ensuring they have a model for each task might help, and completion problems could be particularly effective, since they force students to think, but don't demand much writing. Sam can then try to reduce the guidance he offers, until students are getting started unaided.
- Samira's students don't access revision resources: she could set a clear default about how to begin - "Always begin by quizzing yourself on the most recent unit we finished" - while encouraging students to deviate from them if they can suggest something more important.
- Andy's trainees face "groups of students who are reluctant to take books out of bags and write anything": they could set simple defaults, like putting books on the table and writing the title at the start of the lesson.

(These strategies should help if students are unsure how to begin. As we discuss below, if students don't want to begin, different strategies will be needed.)

Key idea

If students don't know how to start; we can ask ourselves:

- **How can I clarify what students need to do, and how to do it?**
- **Are students struggling to decide how to start? Could a default help?**
- **When can I start to reduce the guidance I offer?**

Our answers may differ between individual students (depending on their knowledge and commitment): Anna needs clear instructions, Amit should be deciding how to start without our input.

Clearer guidance shows students what to do, but it doesn't ensure they feel confident to do it: making the first step easier may help.

4.2 If students don't feel confident to start

Students may know what we want them to do, but lack the confidence to do it. Making the first step easier - or making it seem easier - builds on the approach described in Chapter 1 (breaking tasks into manageable and achievable steps); it goes further by reshaping the initial step to make it more attractive and less intimidating.

We can make the task seem smaller

Usually, we give students the whole task at once, but even if they can do it, a blank page or a series of questions may seem forbidding. We can make a task seem more manageable by revealing its full extent gradually. For example, I struggled to mark books regularly: a pile of thirty books seemed enormous, and I procrastinated. I learned to trick myself into doing it by placing five books in front of me, and leaving the rest on the shelf behind me. Having marked these - taking five minutes at most - I reached behind me for another five. This worked, not just because it broke the task down, but because it hid its true size. Similarly, we can reveal one step or one question at a time (aloud or on the screen), asking students to "Write your first sentence" instead of "Write your answer," or to explain "What will you do first?" rather than "What will you do?" We can also use completion problems: initially, students get a worked example, and need only complete the final step (then the last two steps, and so on). These approaches both encourage students to start (because they look easier) and support learning, by allowing students to focus on one step at a time, limiting the burden on their working memory.[191] (The risk is that students complete a step, stop, and lose confidence or enthusiasm: we can avoid this by introducing the next step rapidly; "Pause, question one is going beautifully, when it's done, move on to question two.")

> *Reveal tasks step by step*

We can start by revisiting past successes

By revisiting past successes, we show students they can succeed again. For example, starting a lesson (or topic) by reviewing students' existing relevant knowledge makes new learning easier,[192] but it also implies the new topic will be manageable: we can begin by posing questions or practising skills all students can manage. We can also show how new tasks resemble others which students have completed successfully: "You did something just like this last lesson" or "You worked non-stop for ten minutes yesterday, I'd like you to do the same again today." This may particularly help with independent tasks: "The first homework question has the same structure as the question we've just done." Finally, we can encourage students to generalise from past success: "You've managed everything in the last three lessons, I'm sure you can manage this." (This is another way to put students in credit, discussed in Chapter 2, encouraging them to maintain their existing level of success.) Our urge is often to move on quickly - but revisiting past successes should convince students they can succeed again.

> *Begin by revising things students have already done*

We can make it hard to get the first task wrong

If it's hard for students to be wrong, it's hard for them to resist starting. Task design can help: initially we can ask for descriptions or opinions rather than correct answers; "What do you see in this picture/text/problem? What could be happening?" Technical skills can be introduced in risk-free ways too: maths teacher Ollie Lovell introduces coordinate systems by asking students to graph fruit as "tasty" (the *x*-axis) and "squishy" (the *y*-axis). We could even ask students to write a bad first sentence or a wrong answer (then improve it). Our words can emphasise this lack of risk too: instead of asking "Why does Macbeth decide to 'proceed no further' in murdering Duncan?" we could ask "Why might Macbeth decide to 'proceed no further' in murdering Duncan?" (This principle applies in managing behaviour too: first asking students to "Listen for a moment," demands less of them than "Calm down and apologise.") We want to get on with the lesson, but making it hard to be wrong initially makes it hard for students to avoid trying: this may save time later.

> Make the first task low risk

Caveat: balance ease and challenge

We must balance imperatives:[193] a thought-provoking task which students won't start is no more use than an appealing task from which they learn nothing. This isn't always a problem: defaults make starting easier, and we can choose defaults which best promote learning; revealing the task gradually makes it seem easier, but doesn't change the task. However, we cannot remove critical elements of the lesson just to encourage students to start, nor can we lose sight of the big picture (breaking down the water cycle is fine, but students need to understand how it fits together too). We need to use "desirable difficulties" too: techniques which force students to think harder and help them to remember better, such as spacing practice (revisiting topics), varying practice (for example, by alternating between different kinds of questions), and gradually reducing guidance and feedback.[194] Finally, making starting easier helps students who are unsure or unconfident: it won't motivate students who are disinterested; they may need more challenge, not less (and we may want to apply the strategies discussed in Chapter 2).

Applications

- Sam described trying to influence "The class that won't work . . . They won't accept the smallest level of challenge." He might pick an initial task he would normally give younger students, which he is sure all his students can manage – then build on their success.
- Samira provides "students with lots of revision resources – they don't access them": she could make the first revision task similar (or identical) to one which students have completed in a previous lesson; students will know what to do, and know they can do it.

- Andy described his trainees facing "groups of students who are reluctant to take books out of bags and write anything." Trainees could ask students to describe pictures, give opinions, or write bad answers: once students have begun to write, trainees can reveal further tasks step by step.

Key idea

Taking the first step creates momentum. We can help students by asking ourselves:

- **Can I introduce instructions and ideas one at a time?**
- **Can I ask students to reprise past successes?**
- **Can I make the first task seem less risky?**

Most of the examples I've given above relate to lesson planning, but we can apply these strategies to plan conversations, units of work, and school years as well. Once students have begun, we can challenge them to take the next step immediately, offering feedback to help them refine their work, and removing support before students become reliant on it. Each step is a building block for the next, helping students both to make progress, and to revise their beliefs about the subject and themselves: they should begin to see themselves as someone who tries – and succeeds (we discuss this idea more fully in Chapter 5). We can reinforce our attempts to clarify what to do, and to convince students they can do it, by using practice.

4.3 If students struggle to start

We can practise tasks before asking students to begin independently

Practising tasks together ensures students know what to do, and experience success, before they begin independently. Effective practice is crucial to developing expertise:[195] its value in increasing skill and confidence has been demonstrated in domains as diverse as medical training,[196] customer service,[197] and preparing for non-violent protest in the Civil Rights movement.[198] Effective practice focuses on specific, sequenced goals:[199] it helps people perfect individual steps, and combine them fluently and confidently under pressure.[200] We can practise:

- Focusing – by practising classroom routines, like looking at the speaker, setting up equipment and packing away: "I've explained how we set up – I'd like to see if you can do it in two minutes."
- Applying the right technique – by practising building blocks (like times tables); individual steps of a procedure (like finding the common denominator); preparing answers before writing them in books (aloud or on whiteboards); and deciding what technique to apply to answer a question.

- Contributing – by asking students to practise what they will say with a partner, and by practising routines, like taking turns and disagreeing politely.

(Practice can mean mental rehearsal too: students could imagine a challenging exam question or difficult social situation, and how to resolve it.) Practice ensures students know exactly what to do, and shows them that they can do it (while allowing us to review their efforts and offer feedback). Any time we want students to do something new – or better – practice prepares them to succeed independently.

> *Practise new tasks together before asking students to complete them independently*

Practice helps students by encoding success, making getting things right feel familiar, then habitual.[201] (This is what distinguishes effective practice from rehearsal, in which things may go well – or not.) This has two implications: first, we want students to get things right almost all the time, so while practice should be challenging, if students struggle, we should make it slightly easier (then make it harder again). Second, because practice encodes success, more practice is an effective and motivating way to respond whenever students struggle with a task (it's probably more effective than repeating our instructions or giving a sanction).[202] We can address a common error with a fifteen-second practice task (rather than a reminder): "We struggled spelling 'beautiful,' so please close your book, take your whiteboard, and write it now," or "A couple of people were slow to put their pens down to listen . . . pick up your pens again . . . and put them down and eyes on me in three, two and one." We can address bigger issues with practice activities: "Our accuracy in using tenses is slipping: please write one thing you did yesterday and one thing you'll do tomorrow, using this model to help." And we can design our systems to encode success: at Ashcroft Technology Academy, students who are referred to senior leaders for poor behaviour face a sanction, such as a detention, but they must also return to the teacher with whom they misbehaved, and complete their work to the teacher's satisfaction. Whenever students struggle, practice is an effective way to start building habits of success.

> *Practise until students succeed*

Caveat: Make practice increasingly difficult

We want students to encode success, but we also want to prepare them for realistic challenges: as they succeed, we need to make practice progressively harder. Academically, we can reduce our support, ask harder questions, and vary the techniques students need to use to answer them. Behaviourally, we can combine tasks – "This time I'd like you to pack up the equipment, and your things, in sixty seconds" – and practise increasingly challenging social scenarios: "You run into Mark on the bus: what's the first thing you'll say . . . Mark gives you an unpleasant look, how will you react?" Once students have started, we can prepare them for success by making practice harder and more realistic.

> *Make practice harder*

Applications

- Sam described trying to influence "The class that won't work ... They won't accept the smallest level of challenge." He could practise simple tasks with them until students are responding automatically, starting with verbal questions and ensuring students are able – and accustomed – to answering quickly and accurately, then moving on to short writing tasks.
- Samira provides "students with lots of revision resources – they don't access them": she could practise revision activities with students in lessons.
- Andy described his trainees facing "groups of students who are reluctant to take books out of bags and write anything": he could practise classroom routines like taking books out swiftly; or practise what he wants them to write aloud or on mini whiteboards before asking students to record it in their books.

Key idea

We can ensure students can start, and feel confident doing so, by practising – before they begin independent work, and whenever they struggle. We can ask:

- **What do students need to practise to be able to start independently?**
- **What would show me they need further practice?**
- **How can I make practice increasingly challenging and realistic?**

Practice lets students see themselves improve, and lets us highlight their successes (we discuss this further in Chapter 5).

Conclusion

We can make starting easier and more attractive for students by asking:

- How can I clarify what students should do?
- How can I make the first step easier?
- How can I use practice to ensure students are ready?

Making starting easy helps students gain momentum: we need to help them maintain that momentum, while reducing our support and increasing the level of challenge. The next chapter suggests ways to achieve this.

Checklist

I have **s**pecified what I want students to do (based on Chapter 1).
I have **i**nspired and **m**otivated students to do it (based on Chapter 2).
I have helped them **pl**an action (based on Chapter 3).

I help them **i**nitiate action	
1) If students don't know how to start, I . . .	
• Give clear instructions	*"First, book out; then, title and date; then, answer the question."*
• Share models	*"First, examine the model, then see if you can answer this similar question."*
• Set a default	*"If you're unsure what structure to use, use our standard five-mark answer structure."*
2) If students don't feel confident to start, I . . .	
• Make the task seem smaller	*"I only want you to answer the first question, then we'll go over it together."*
• Revisit past successes	*"Today's first question is almost identical to the one you all got right last lesson."*
• Make the first task hard to get wrong	*"First, I want to hear whether you liked the poem."*
3) If students struggle to start, I . . .	
• Ask them to practise	*"Draft the first line, then we'll review them together before you begin independently."*
• Use practice whenever they struggle	*"That wasn't an appropriate way to talk, I'd like you to say that again in a calmer tone of voice."*
Next, I **f**ollow up to help students to keep going (Chapter 5).	

Copyright material from Harry Fletcher-Wood (2022), *Habits of Success: Getting Every Student Learning*, Routledge

Workshop 4: building a culture of achievement

What's the situation?

Ed is struggling with a small group of "in" pupils in his class: they won't engage, announce they're bored, avoid writing, and brag about never reading a book. He's worried that their influence is rippling around the class: many children who love reading feel put off. (He's also finding their behaviour increasingly frustrating.) He wants students to be willing to give learning a go, and to allow others to do their best too. He's already tried everything he can think of, including sanctions, without success. (This situation came from a primary school teacher.)

What would you suggest?

1) What is the fundamental challenge? What habit or steps would solve it?
2) How would you inspire students to act?
3) Do students need to commit to action?
4) How can you make it easy?
5) How can you help students keep going?

Step 1) Specify the change

Ed knows that what he wants to build is a culture of achievement and support - but he also knows that he needs to define what that means if students are going to pursue it. Vague and general requests like encouraging students to "Do your best" or "Be supportive" won't help, since students may interpret them differently. Ed reduces what he wants students to do to two things:

- Start tasks immediately
- Say something positive/supportive before saying anything critical.

He decides to introduce them one at a time, ensuring students are starting work before trying to change how they talk about it.

Step 2) Inspire and motivate students

Ed recognises that he's unlikely to convince students by demanding action, or telling them it's a good idea. He asks students who their role models are - and whether they delay starting tasks. He emphasises social norms, both within the classroom (most students start quickly) and across the school. Finally, he highlights an immediate cost of inaction: the risk of not getting to break on time. (He makes similar points to encourage students to say positive things, but also asks them to reflect on how they feel about negative comments, helping them to recognise the problem he hopes to overcome.) Ed doesn't expect to convince all his students, but he thinks it's worth trying.

Step 3) Plan change

Even if students are swayed by his arguments, Ed doubts they'll be willing to commit to change explicitly. Nonetheless, he tells students about each change the week before he intends to introduce it, and plans simple reminders he can use frequently: "Jess is about to make a positive comment, then maybe a criticism, Jess . . . ."

Step 4) Initiate action

Ed has warned students, but he anticipates that the change could still come as a shock to some. He removes every conceivable barrier to getting started. For every task, he shows students a model, then gives clear, simple instructions about what he wants them to do. He sets a default which removes any excuse for inaction: if students are unsure how to answer a question, they must keep writing while they wait for help – even if what they write is inaccurate, incorrect or off-topic. (He recognises potential disadvantages, but initially, he just wants students to get into the habit of writing. This should allow him to spend less time firefighting, and more time helping.) And he asks students to script possible positive comments, and practise giving them to one another in a sincere tone.

Step 5) Follow up

One minute after each independent task begins, Ed pauses and scans the room to check how many students are writing. Whenever the numbers are higher than normal, he highlights this. He gives students rapid feedback about their comments, asking the class "Did that comment include a positive before the negative?" If not, he invites the student to try again. Over time, he tries to emphasise that these habits reflect who the class are: a kind and hard-working group. As the term comes to an end, he considers relaunching the habits, with an added emphasis on the accuracy and quality of students' written and spoken answers.

Conclusion

Ed had thought he would meet significant resistance – but many students respond willingly to his clear, simple requests. He successfully removes almost every possible reason for less willing students not to get started: faced with clear guidance and an increasingly positive social norm, their apparent resistance evaporates, and they begin to start tasks habitually. This creates a far more positive classroom environment, and allows Ed to focus on helping students improve, not just on getting them started.

5 How can we help students to keep going?

Specify the change: pick a priority, then choose a powerful habit or small step to achieve it

Inspire and motivate students to value the change

PLan change: ask students to commit to action

Initiate action: make starting easy

Follow up: help students keep going

Chapter map: how can we help students to keep going?

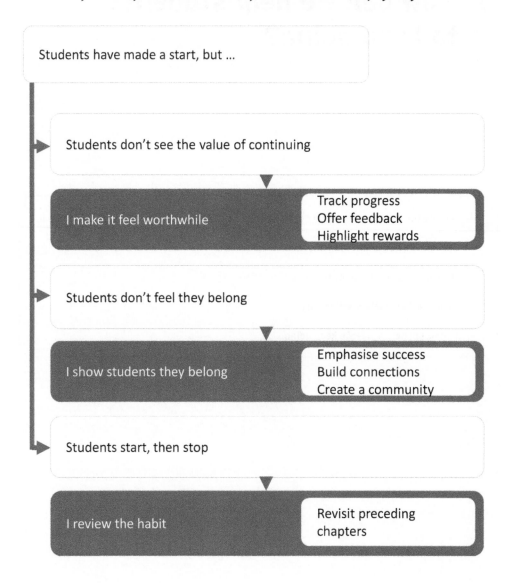

Students have made a start, but …

Students don't see the value of continuing

I make it feel worthwhile
- Track progress
- Offer feedback
- Highlight rewards

Students don't feel they belong

I show students they belong
- Emphasise success
- Build connections
- Create a community

Students start, then stop

I review the habit
- Revisit preceding chapters

I give students increasing autonomy and more challenging goals

Copyright material from Harry Fletcher-Wood (2022), *Habits of Success: Getting Every Student Learning*, Routledge

The problem

Sustaining change is crucial: students succeed through habits of attention and effort, not occasional bursts of effort. But helping students form positive habits is hard:

- Busra's class worked "fairly well in my lessons but only for short periods on written work, and they need a lot of support." Two boys seemed to require near constant one-to-one support: "as soon as I leave one of them to continue independently they stop writing until I return, which I can't do until I have got the rest of the class back on task." She wanted them to be able to do written work independently "for 5-7 minutes so I can attend to others who are genuinely stuck."
- Joel gave his maths class weekly readings, questions and a low-stakes quiz, but "Not many of them are keeping up with the programme and I see very little improvement overall on the quizzes."
- Michael was struggling to get his A level students reading for twenty minutes every day, and sharing their thoughts about their reading.

Situations like these can make us question whether it's possible to get all students learning sustainably - but if we've managed to get them started, there are several ways we can keep them going.

The principle: follow up to help students build habits

Students sustain change by forming habits: to support this, we can help them to recognise the value of continuing, and to feel that they belong; if they falter, we can relaunch the habit.

A person forms a habit by repeating a rewarding action in a specific situation (a place, a time, or a social situation, for example).[203] With enough repetition, the situation becomes the cue to act:[204] if students make a plan every time they see a tricky question, a tricky question comes to cue a plan, and they have formed a habit. Strategies suggested in previous chapters contribute to forming habits:

- Specifying a powerful habit (discussed in Chapter 1) helps because it's easier to make simpler actions habitual.[205]
- Showing the value of learning (Chapter 2) helps because people need a reason to start forming a habit.
- When students plan when and where to act (Chapter 3), they choose the situation which will come to cue the habit.
- Practice offers repetition, which means students are beginning to form a habit (Chapter 4).

Nonetheless, as the problems described above show, getting started is not enough: we need students to keep going for long enough to form a habit. We can help them by highlighting what they're achieving, by making them feel they belong - and by relaunching the habit when they falter.

5.1 If students don't see the value of continuing

We can help students to see the value of continuing by tracking their progress, offering feedback, and making it feel rewarding.

We can track students' progress in forming a habit

Often, we go "fishing" in the classroom: we scan the room, or look at students' work, without seeking anything specific.[206] If we are to offer useful support and meaningful feedback however, we must know what progress students are making with the habit we have prioritised. It's hard to monitor this and simultaneously attend to everything else they are doing, so we need a systematic approach: a simple, observable and valid measure of the habit we want students to form. For example:

If our priority is . . .	And students' goal is . . .	We can track . . .
Focus	To work uninterrupted	How many students are working independently. How long an individual/group can work uninterrupted.
Applying the right technique	To begin a question the right way without support	How many students begin the question in the right way. How many students use specific techniques unprompted.
Perseverance	To overcome difficulties independently	How many students check their work against the model when they're stuck. How far students get on a difficult task. How many students complete their homework.
Contribution	Contributing to discussions	How many students contribute to discussion during the lesson.

These measures are intentionally simple: we're not trying to record how good every student's contribution is (for example); we're trying to track whether our efforts to encourage students to contribute (our priority) are working. (If students begin to contribute regularly, we could then prioritise - and track - their ability to make more sophisticated contributions, which build on their peers' comments.) We should apply the measure simply too: for example, ticking names on a class list or seating plan shows at a glance who has written a good opening sentence, contributed to a discussion or used a specific technique. A simple measure, simply applied, shows whether students are beginning to form a habit.

> *Pick a simple measure of students' progress in forming a habit, and a simple way to apply it*

We could underestimate the power of such measures: we monitor students' work already, and we know roughly how well they are doing. But picking one measure allows us to check rapidly whether all students are forming the desired habit: we can review thirty opening sentences – and decide what support students need – far faster than we can review thirty paragraphs. Additionally, systematic approaches can surprise us: ticking a class list may reveal that more (or fewer) students are contributing than we had thought; that one student is doing unusually well, while another has been unobtrusively silent. Focusing on a single measure may feel limiting, since there are so many things we want students to improve, but while it helps us to focus, it doesn't preclude us from also offering more detailed individual feedback. If we are confident we have prioritised the most important habit, we should focus on it until students master it: helping students persevere before we worry about how much they are contributing to the lesson, for example (as we discussed in Chapter 1). Simple measures demonstrate whether students are forming habits: this guides our feedback and support.

> *A measure focuses our attention: this allows us to focus our support*

Picking a clear measure – and describing it to the class – helps students too. First, saying what we're looking for clarifies what we expect (and emphasises that it matters): "You must find the common denominator before adding fractions – that's what I'm checking." People are more likely to act desirably if they know someone may check:[207] telling students "I'm coming around to ensure everyone has got beyond Question 2" shows we care, and gives students a standard to reach and an incentive to reach it. Students can use our measure to monitor and regulate their actions too:[208] "Review the questions you got wrong: did you find a common denominator first?" Once students have formed one habit, we can pick a new habit and measure (to ensure students don't fixate on one aspect of success), while occasionally checking they are maintaining the existing one.

> *A clear measure encourages students to act and helps them regulate their actions*

We can offer feedback

Feedback highlighting a gap between current and desired performance encourages students to close that gap.[209] We can convey the gap, without being critical, by describing what our measure shows students are doing (and not doing): "Two thirds of you have completed Question 1," "I've heard from half the class in today's discussion," "That's the third time you've called out." Displaying progress visually has a similar effect: we could tick off how many questions students have attempted, or how many homeworks they have completed, on a board; or we could ask students to record their progress on a checklist. These approaches reinforce social norms (discussed in Chapter 2): if students know most of their peers have contributed, this suggests that they can, and should, do so too. If they miss the implication, we can be more explicit: "I've heard from half the class already – I'd like to hear from everyone by the end of the lesson." Describing what students have done may encourage them to do more.

Describing what our measure shows may encourage students to do more

We can offer feedback, not just about what students are doing, but about how they can do better. When we do however, our aim is not to provide feedback – it's to help students make a change: to use a different technique, or contribute in a new way, for example. To help students change, our feedback must apply the strategies described in previous chapters; prioritising the most important change (Chapter 1), convincing students it matters (Chapter 2), and providing clear guidance, models, and practice (Chapter 4). For example, if we want students to improve the way they answer a question, we might pick a crucial misconception, show why it matters, model a better answer, then ask students to practise. In other words, effective feedback – feedback which leads students to change what they do – follows the steps set out in this book. Given this, examining feedback here would repeat much of, and add little to, what has been covered already. (Readers can find a summary of the evidence on feedback and its classroom applications in Chapter 6 of my previous book, *Responsive Teaching*.) Feedback can contribute one more thing to keeping students going however – it can help students recognise their progress. We discuss this in the next section.

Feedback about how to improve means helping students change: it means applying the strategies covered in previous chapters

We can make it rewarding

People are more likely to keep doing something if they find it rewarding. Ideally, students would be intrinsically motivated: they would see what they are doing as rewarding in itself. However, a task can be valuable without being intrinsically motivating, and students' intrinsic motivation falls each year they are in school.[210] First, therefore, we discuss extrinsic rewards: rewards which we offer. Most schools and most teachers have a reward system – but behavioural science suggests several ways in which these systems could be refined to encourage students to keep going, and form habits.

Offering rewards

WHAT TO OFFER

Rewards can help people form habits. For example, researchers offered people $175 to go to the gym twice a week for a month. Unsurprisingly, most participants went. More importantly, afterwards they kept going: the reward encouraged them to go enough times that they formed a habit. (Another group – who described themselves as equally enthusiastic about exercise – received $175, but only had to go the gym once. They didn't keep going: it was the reward - not their motivation - which created the habit.)[211] Researchers have motivated students using a range of rewards, including prizes, tokens, certificates and money;[212] the chance to win a big prize might work too.[213] *What* we offer doesn't seem particularly important: it could be anything students want, including the school's merits or reward points, our own system of stickers or prizes, or "lottery tickets" for a draw at the end of term. But experiments in schools have found varying effects: some positive, some neutral, some negative.[214] It's *when*, *how* and *why* we offer rewards that makes a difference: rewards work best when they are a pleasant surprise after a specific action.

> *It doesn't matter what rewards we offer (provided they're tempting): what matters is when, how and why we offer them*

WHAT TO REWARD

Rewards work when they encourage students to take specific actions, and so build habits. For example, researchers offered students money for getting higher test scores. Students were enthusiastic, but they didn't know how to get higher scores, so the rewards had no effect.[215] In the same study, other students were offered money to read books - these students did gain higher test scores.[216] Rewarding specific habits of success (like reading books, or revising) is more effective than rewarding success itself (such as test scores):[217] students must know exactly what to keep doing.[218] So our rewards should be as specific as our priorities and our measures: we should reward focusing for ten minutes, not working hard for a week; completing practice questions at home, not getting full marks on a test; making a thoughtful contribution to the lesson, not being constructive throughout it. We should reward specific actions - our rewards should not, however, be predictable.

> *Reward specific actions - not overall performance*

WHEN TO GIVE REWARDS

"Surprisingly, habits form best when rewards are powerful enough to motivate behavior but are uncertain in the sense that they do not always occur."[219] In general, consistency and predictability help in schools: students need to know what to expect. However, consistent, predictable rewards have diminishing effects: students may come to see them as an entitlement, regardless of their effort, or they may work for the reward alone,[220] only trying when one is offered. Rewards which are a pleasant surprise - which are unpredictable - motivate repetition and habit formation by encouraging people to focus on what they hope will happen:

> People keep paying money into [slot] machines because sometimes they win, sometimes they don't . . . E-mail and social networking sites have similar effects: people keep checking on them because sometimes they are rewarded with interesting communications, but other times they get only junk. The key is that rewards are received probabilistically, meaning not for every behavior.[221]

A predictable reward might help initially – paying people to go to the gym helped them form a habit – but once students have begun, an occasional reward is likely to be more effective. For example, if we want students to do their homework, we might give every student a merit for completing it in the first three weeks of term, then surprise them with another merit in week six. (Once we have decided to reward students, we should do so as soon as possible: immediate rewards motivated students to work harder, but rewards announced immediately and distributed a month later had no effect.)[222] So when we give rewards effectively – when we offer a pleasant surprise for a specific action – we may say something like: "That was such a thoughtful suggestion that I'm going to give you a merit (sticker/bookmark/lottery ticket)."

Make rewards a pleasant surprise

Monitoring the effects

We must monitor the effects rewards have: we may need to alter our approach to ensure students benefit. Effects vary, and are hard to predict: for example, some studies have found girls respond better to rewards, others boys; some have seen higher-attaining students benefit more, others lower-attainers.[223] Effects can be positive and negative: one study found prizes motivated high attainers, but demotivated low attainers;[224] another found that rewarding students for doing their maths homework made them better at maths, but worse at reading.[225] Finally, students could infer that we are offering a reward because the action is difficult, or unattractive: they may stop trying if we stop offering rewards, or pursue the reward, not the action we're encouraging.[226] We can try to overcome these problems by changing the criteria for getting the reward. For example, my Sixth Form students were motivated to attend by their Educational Maintenance Allowance payments, but they were paid for attending promptly for a full week: if they were late on Monday, some students made a point of being late all week; "I've lost my EMA, there's no point." A simple change would have avoided this: offering £5 per day, and a bonus for the week, rather than one weekly payment. Similarly, if students seem unmoved by rewards, we can change what we reward: "From now on, I'll be rewarding your personal best effort," for example. (We may also consider changing how students receive the reward: teenagers may dislike being singled out as successful in front of their peers;[227] but researchers found they were motivated by certificates sent to their parents.)[228] Monitoring the effects rewards are having – and redesigning our approach accordingly – is essential.

Monitor the effects of rewards; redesign them if necessary

Highlighting intrinsic rewards

If students see their actions as intrinsically rewarding – as worthwhile and meaningful in their own right – they don't need extrinsic rewards: encouragement and support are enough to keep them going.[229] Making progress with meaningful tasks is satisfying:[230] we can ask students to stop frequently and recognise what they've achieved; "Look at the question you've just answered - none of you could do that at the beginning of the lesson." We can also prompt them to recognise the value of what they've learned: one study did this by asking students to describe how the science unit they had just completed could be "useful to you, or a friend/relative, in daily life? How does learning about this topic apply to your future plans?"[231] One student wrote:

> Graphing is important part of life (sic.) because when you're trying to compare different data the graph is the best way to go. For an example, my grandmother and aunt work at a retirement home and they need to decide dosages per day, meals, and etc.[232]

This prompt increased interest in science (among students who did not expect to do well), and students later got higher grades (than a control group, who just reviewed the topic). Any time students succeed, we can highlight how their action is either immediately valuable, or contributes to a more distant goal: "How could this help you later in the lesson/in life?" Prompting students to recognise what they've achieved, and why it matters, encourages them to keep going; it may also influence their self-belief and identity, the subject of the next section.

> *Help students see that they're making progress, and that it matters*

Applications

- Busra struggled with two boys who seemed to require near constant one-to-one support: she could track their actions - or have them track their own actions - by putting a stopwatch beside them and asking them to monitor how long they can work independently. She could also offer rewards - initially for every three-minute burst of independent work, then as a surprise when students do particularly well.
- Joel's students weren't keeping up with questions and readings: he asked them to create electronic flash cards, allowing them - and him - to monitor how much they were doing (and encouraging competition between them).
- Michael wanted students to read every day: he could track how many books students have read (perhaps on a wall chart), rewarding them occasionally (perhaps for reading a particularly interesting or tricky book). He could also emphasise the intrinsic value of reading, asking how what they have read has helped them make sense of the course.

Key idea

We can encourage students to keep going - to form a habit - by tracking their actions, offering feedback and rewards, and highlighting progress, and its value. To do so effectively, we must ask ourselves:

- **How do I know what progress students are making in forming a habit?**

- **How do students know how well they're doing and what they need to do next?**
- **Can I surprise students with a tempting reward for a specific action?**
- **What effects are rewards having?**
- **How can I help students see the value of their actions?**

Tracking students' actions also reveals how students are changing: it allows us to help them build an identity as successful individuals and members of a community.

5.2 If students don't feel they belong

People's identities - how they see themselves and what they feel part of - powerfully influence what they do: Spurs fans don't wear Arsenal shirts. If students believe they are hardworking (and feel part of the class), they are more likely to start, and to keep going. We introduce identity late in the book for two reasons. First, focusing initially on how students see themselves distracts us from their actions. Their actions matter more. For example, if students avoid writing and lack confidence, increasing their confidence is difficult and uncertain (have we convinced them or are they just saying so?). If we succeed, students may feel confident to write, but still avoid doing it. Better to get students writing (by making it easy to begin, for example) than to build their confidence, hoping they will write. Second, we can best influence students' beliefs *once they have started*, because people's habits and successes shape how they see themselves:[233] "I'm writing well - I guess I can succeed." Having reached Chapter 5, I hope your students have made a good start: this will allow us to show them that they belong, as successful individuals, and as part of a community.

> *Get students started, then show them what their success signifies*

We can build students' identities

If students are to see themselves as mathematicians, hard workers or good citizens, they must:

1) **Succeed:** the strategies discussed in preceding chapters are designed to get students started. Success increases people's confidence, and encourages them to keep going:[234] meaningful self-belief depends on students' success.
2) **Recognise their success:** students may overlook or discount their successes; we can encourage them to pause and recognise what they've achieved.[235] Students could assess themselves,[236] or we could guide them (teachers who reviewed students' successes each day saw their mathematical confidence increase).[237] We can emphasise progress:

   - During a task: by highlighting how much students have got right, for example, ticking every correct step rather than just ticking the final answer.[238]
   - Between tasks: "Before we start writing, take a moment and note three new ideas you've understood from the text."

However, students' confidence is lowest in the moment;[239] so they may find it easier to recognise their success:

- After a task: "Look back at your last three essays: what has improved?"
- At milestones: completing a task the first time feels momentous; creating subsequent milestones can help students recognise their continued improvement – their fifth essay, tenth homework, hundredth correct times table.[240]

3) **Attribute their success to their efforts:** if students believe they succeeded due to luck, their beliefs about what they can do and who they are won't change; we must help them see how their effort and skill have helped. We could ask them to "Write one thing you did that helped you complete this successfully," or ask broader questions after longer periods of success: "You've been focusing hard all term, what have you learned about how to concentrate well?"

4) **See that their success means something:** as students try, and succeed, we can encourage them to recognise – and name – the strengths they are developing. Students might realise that their efforts reflect "perseverance," that they are showing the "diligence of a scientist," or the characteristics of a role model: the "curiosity of Darwin," for example.

We can then draw on the beliefs students have developed about themselves to encourage them to keep going. For example, (using strategies we discussed in Chapter 2) we can invite students to stay in credit ("You've contributed brilliantly all term, keep it up this week"), to see themselves as role models ("Think about what's helped you – what would you advise Year 5?"), and to see success as personally meaningful ("The final assessment builds on all your hard work this term: please revise thoroughly").

> *Help students recognise their success, recognise what it says about them, and then maintain it*

We can create a sense of belonging

People want to belong:[241]

> We love to join teams, clubs, leagues, and fraternities. We take on group identities and work shoulder to shoulder with strangers so enthusiastically that it seems our minds were designed for teamwork . . . . We are not saints, but we are sometimes good team players.[242]

The pride, loyalty and belonging people feel as part of a group makes them happier and more motivated; they willingly transcend self-interest, doing things they wouldn't do for themselves alone.[243] How can we convince students they belong?

Connecting students

We can begin to create a community by helping students connect to their peers. People like and support others more when they have something in common, even something as trivial as a birthday or favourite band.[244] Teenage National Citizen Service participants trusted others more after spending ten minutes identifying what their group had in common (compared to groups who discussed other topics, like their differences).[245] We could help a group to bond, or a new student to integrate, by asking students to identify their similarities. Taking others' perspectives can overcome existing differences: Israeli and Palestinian teenagers, for example, are introduced in person, in writing or on video, then asked to imagine one another's feelings, or to take one another's perspectives. They see each other more positively – and act accordingly – as a result.[246] If connecting students is proving difficult, asking students to imagine or describe a peer's feelings could help. Emphasising what students have in common, and asking them to take one another's perspectives, should help them connect to one another.

> *Help students to see their similarities to their peers, and their peers' points of view*

Connecting students and teachers

We can also try to deepen our connection with students. In one study, researchers asked teachers and students to fill in the same questionnaire, and highlighted what they had in common. This led teachers to like their students more, to interact more with minority students and to give them higher grades.[247] Seeking and highlighting things we have in common with students – interests, sibling relationships, school experiences – may improve our relationships with them. We can also emphasise that students belong at critical moments. One such moment is the start of the lesson: welcoming students at the door improves subsequent behaviour.[248] Another is giving feedback, which students often see as critical or threatening. One study added a handwritten message to teachers' normal written marking which read: "I'm giving you these comments because I have very high expectations and I know that you can reach them."[249] Minority students who received this message were more likely to edit and resubmit their work, gained higher grades, and trusted the school more. To help students feel they belong in our class we can highlight what we have in common, and defuse moments of tension by expressing warmth, high standards and a belief that students can meet them.[250]

> *Highlight what we have in common with students, and emphasise they belong when they may doubt it*

Building a community

Communities form when people behave in similar ways, share values, and "feel like a family."[251] Our language can convey communal feeling, both through pronouns ("we" rather than "you") and adjectives: describing a maths department in supportive terms made it seem more welcoming, and made students work harder at maths tasks;[252] we could emphasise that "we are a supportive, hard-working class." Coordinated activity creates a feeling of shared purpose and identity (think of the Haka):[253] forming choirs or organising dance competitions between classes or year groups could help.[254] And communities are distinguished by the rituals they use to mark transitions and prepare people for new roles, such as graduations, weddings and funerals.[255] Silkwood School uses festivals and ceremonies to "unite the school community": students' completion of primary school is marked by "a journey festival moving [students] from the primary campus onto the High School site with the primary school students saying farewell and the High School students welcoming them to the new and next stage of their learning adventure."[256] We can develop rituals as a school – a "graduation" at the end of each year for students and their families, for example – and as a class, like applause each time a student improves a personal best. We can create a community through collective language, activity and rituals.

> *Collective language, activities and rituals create a community*

As individuals within a community

Belonging to a community is powerful, but students must feel that they matter as individuals within it. Simply telling them they belong can help: one school sent students postcards when they were absent, which read, "We missed you today"; one student responded "I didn't know it mattered I was gone. I missed you too. Thank you for that note. It made me feel special."[257] Another powerful approach is self-affirmation: asking individuals to write about values which matter to them (this increases their sense of security when they are in an unfamiliar environment, and are being asked to change).[258] For example, researchers asked new students to write about values which mattered to them (like friendship, and family): African-American students gained confidence, got higher grades and were less likely to repeat a year (compared to students who wrote about values which were not important to them); the effects were strongest among lower-performing students.[259] We can remind students they belong; we can emphasise it by asking them to write about their values – perhaps as a brief tutorial activity.

> *Show students they belong as individuals within the community*

Applications

- Busra struggled with two boys who seemed to require near constant one-to-one support: she could highlight every bit of progress they make, helping them to see themselves as focused and independent – then draw on this belief to encourage further effort.
- Joel's students aren't keeping up with questions and readings: he could ask students to support one another (perhaps finding questions they are all struggling with); he could also emphasise that the questions are a way to ensure the whole group succeeds, and no one falls behind.
- Michael wanted students to read every day: he could ask groups of students to read the same book, and could emphasise that he is encouraging reading because he wants students to do well, and believes they can.

Key idea

We may feel uncomfortable seeking to influence individual or group identities;[260] collective activities and rituals can feel empty or forced.[261] But all high-performing teams develop and rely upon a collective spirit and collaborative ethos, celebrating success, and developing private jokes and traditions. If we want students to feel individually successful – and part of a community – we may ask:

- How can I help students recognise what they have achieved?
- How can I help students see what they have in common?
- How can I deepen my connection with students?
- How can I help students feel part of a community?
- How can I help students feel individually important within the community?

The pride and loyalty this engenders should help students form and maintain habits. Nonetheless, new habits may not stick; we may need to relaunch them.

5.3 If students start, then stop

People form habits slowly and falteringly. It took two months, on average, for people to form a new health habit, such as drinking a glass of water after lunch.[262] Our students may take longer: the goals are tougher (focusing consistently, not just drinking water); prompts are weaker (occasional history lessons, not lunch every day); and students may be discouraged by their peers.[263] Moreover, people initiate new habits, then revert to old ones:[264] for example, one study helped students go to the gym regularly, but a month's holiday broke the habit.[265] Our instinct, when students struggle, may be to assume our approach isn't working. But students are likely to form habits slowly; they may improve then regress; they may stop trying if they struggle: they need time and support. We should review the habit entirely however:

- If students aren't increasingly successful: we can't expect immediate success, but we must see gradual improvement.
- At breaks in routine, like holidays, and periods of pressure, like exams: routines slip, students' priorities change, and we cannot offer as much support.
- At opportunities for a fresh start, such as the new term, and new year (discussed in Chapter 3).

These situations are prompts to review what we have tried, identify barriers, and redesign the change (the checklist summarising the book, on page 135, may help). If we ask students about habit formation, we should get honest responses about the barriers (not just excuses and promises): we can ask, for example, whether a reminder helped, rather than why students didn't do their homework. Having reviewed our approach, and students' experiences, we can relaunch the change, keeping aspects which have worked and improving those which have not. Primarily, we will draw on the strategies discussed in previous chapters: below, we discuss additional considerations when relaunching a habit.

Review the habit when students struggle

Revisiting Chapter 1: is the change right?

As we review the change we have chosen, we may realise we have been too ambitious. We want students to form habits: they will do so by attaining small goals consistently (not by attaining big goals occasionally); it's better to ensure students can focus perfectly for two minutes than have them focus partially for five.[266] Perhaps we prioritised one challenge, but have found another is more fundamental: we want students to make thoughtful contributions, but their contributions are weak because they are struggling to approach problems in the right way. If so, we can prioritise the more fundamental challenge. Alternatively, the priority may be appropriate but the goal too difficult: we are asking students to write elegant paragraphs, but they are struggling to write clear opening sentences. Finally, we may be able to increase students' autonomy: if they are working well, we can ask them to do so more independently, for example. Once we're confident we're pursuing the right change, we can remind students why it matters.

Review the priority: it may be too ambitious

Revisiting Chapter 2: are students willing to begin?

Motivation ebbs: people need to be reminded of – and reengaged by – what motivated them initially.[267] Students may simply need a reminder: we can revisit any of the strategies described in Chapter 2 briefly at the start of any task or lesson. However, asking students to remind us may be better than our reminding them: "Who can tell me the problem that this approach overcomes?" When we revisit the reasons for change, we can highlight the results of students' previous efforts: new norms – "Everyone focused beautifully last lesson"; role models – "See how Ali has refined his answer"; and frames – "You persevered beautifully last week, don't let it slip today." We could also discuss factors that sap motivation: "I struggle to run when it's wet and cold; you may find it harder to focus when you're tired."

Revisit motives in the light of students' achievements

Revisiting Chapter 3: is the plan working?

Students' plans could be too optimistic: they may need different deadlines, new reminders, or alternative forms of support. If their timetable or after-school activities change, their plans will need to change too. We might ask them, "If Tuesday isn't working for homework, when would be better?" Hopefully, they will use the strategies we have taught, responding with something like: "I know I need a memorable prompt, and I want to start when I'm fresh, so I'll begin immediately after breakfast."

Help students revise their commitments

Revisiting Chapter 4: do students need more practice?

If students are struggling to begin, more practice could help. Repetition is essential for habit formation: we could simply practise more, or we could focus on critical aspects; practising choosing which technique to apply to different questions, for example (without actually answering the questions). If we have identified specific barriers, practice is a good way to address them: English teacher Josh Goodrich found students were revising at home, but didn't know how to improve wrong answers; he practised this in lessons until he was confident they could do it independently. More practice can help students form habits – particularly if we focus on the biggest barriers they face.

> *Keep practising – focusing on the hardest elements of the habit*

Revisiting Chapter 5: keep refining

Once students have regained momentum, we can emphasise that their second attempt has been more successful than the first: we want them to recognise that – while they may struggle – they can still succeed. We have discussed how habits are prompted by a situation: being consistent in what we ask students to do (and when, and how, and where) helps them form habits. Ultimately however, we want students to perform well everywhere (not just for us, in our classroom, at certain times): if students are doing well, we could vary the situation (changing the seating plan, for example, or varying when in the lesson we ask students to write), so that they learn to perform well whenever necessary. Finally, we can reduce our input, helping students to succeed autonomously. Then, we can move on to the next challenge.

> *Emphasise students' success, keep refining, then move on to the next challenge*

Applications

- Busra struggled with two boys who seemed to require near constant one-to-one support: every lesson is a chance to relaunch her approach, tweaking goals, prompts, and reminders, until they work.
- Joel's students aren't keeping up with questions and readings: he could ask students where they're struggling, and practise aspects which they are finding difficult.
- Michael wanted students to read every day: he might use a fresh term to revisit the value of reading, and to help them identify better times and places to read.

Key idea

Students' struggles usually reflect how hard forming a habit is, not their inability to succeed. But we can "restart things forever,"[268] refining our approach until the habit sticks, by asking:

- **Is the goal too ambitious?**
- **Do students recall why this matters?**
- **Are students' plans working?**
- **Do they need more practice?**
- **What is the next refinement?**

When we relaunch a habit, we must try to muster the same optimism and enthusiasm with which we began. A relaunch is also a chance to teach students the science of habit formation, both to encourage them to persist and to prepare them to apply these strategies themselves.

Conclusion

Habits of success get students learning - consistently. We can support students to form them by asking:

- How can I show students the value of their progress?
- How can I convince students they belong?
- When do I need to relaunch the habit?

When a habit sticks, we can help students improve further in three ways. First, we can help them to refine the existing habit: to keep persevering, for example, but to adopt new strategies to use when they get stuck. Second, we can reduce our support, giving students increasing control over their learning. Third, we can take up a fresh challenge.

Checklist

I have **s**pecified what I want students to do (based on Chapter 1). I have **i**nspired and **m**otivated students to do it (based on Chapter 2). I have helped them **pl**an action (based on Chapter 3). I have helped them **i**nitiate action (based on Chapter 4).	
I help them keep going by following up	
1) If students don't see the value of continuing, I ...	
• Track students' progress	*Counting how many students begin learning immediately when they enter the room.*
• Offer feedback	*Sharing what I have noticed with students.*
• Surprise students with rewards for specific actions	*Occasionally giving students merits for the habit.*
• Highlight intrinsic rewards	*"What has been satisfying about what you've done?"*
2) If students don't feel they belong, I ...	
• Emphasise students' success, and its significance	*Asking students what they've achieved this term and how it's changed them.*
• Build connections between students and with teachers	*Helping students see what they have in common with each other/teachers.*
• Build a community through collective activity	*Celebrating students' achievements together.*
3) If students start, then stop, I ...	
• Review the change	*Considering whether it's too difficult. Checking or asking what the barriers are.*
• Revisit its value	*Showing students that the class is working harder and test scores are improving as a result.*
• Review the plan	*Asking students to pick a better time to study and a different person to remind them.*
• Offer more practice	*Asking students to write non-stop for two minutes.*
• Keep refining	*Keep tweaking until students succeed consistently.*
Next, I increase students' autonomy and tackle a new challenge.	

Copyright material from Harry Fletcher-Wood (2022), *Habits of Success: Getting Every Student Learning*, Routledge

Workshop 5: getting all students to school on time

What's the situation?

Attendance at Aisha's school has never exceeded the national or local average, and has dipped further this year: she is responsible for increasing it. The school does everything that might be expected, monitoring attendance, calling home to check on unexplained absence, and following up with persistent absentees. This has helped, but too many students are still late or absent each day. Aisha doesn't have enough staff time to organise more intensive support for occasional absentees and latecomers, and she worries that punitive measures will do more harm than good. (Several teachers asked to see how behavioural science could be applied to this situation.)

What would you suggest?

1) What is the fundamental challenge? What habit or steps would solve it?
2) How would you inspire students to act?
3) Do students need to commit to action?
4) How can you make it easy?
5) How can you help students keep going?

Step 1) Specify the change

In one sense, Aisha's goal is simple: she wants students to attend more, and arrive promptly. She hopes that attending will prove rewarding: seeing friends and making progress should encourage students to keep coming back. However, Aisha recognises that this may not work for some students: their first day back reminds them of everything they've missed, socially and academically. She needs to ensure that returning students have a good experience and want to keep coming. Aisha also worries about the many factors which contribute to students' absence and lateness: transport, disorganisation, caring responsibilities, lack of support, and lack of motivation to attend. What works for one student may not help another. Finally, Aisha wants the school to remain compassionate: a percentage target does not justify preventing individual students from attending crucial family events, for example. Aisha adopts two maxims to guide her approach:

- "Every day, a great day" - every day must feel sufficiently worthwhile that students want to come back the next.
- "No barrier overlooked" - something can be done about every barrier students face, whether by Aisha, her colleagues, parents, or other services.

Step 2) Inspire and motivate students

Aisha wants to make "every day a great day" without making substantial demands of her colleagues. She asks them to do two things to conclude each lesson: first, to spend ninety seconds reviewing what students achieved; to describe, or have students describe, what they now understand and can do. Aisha hopes this will help students recognise the immediate benefits of attending. Second, to give students something to look forward to about the next lesson: to offer a hook, a problem to be solved, or an immediate benefit. Aisha hopes that these changes will prove manageable for teachers: they fit any subject and don't require any additional planning. Together, they should show students that they are making progress, and give them a reason to return the next day.

Aisha also offers students role models. The school highlights the achievements of students with full attendance and high grades, but Aisha worries they may not seem similar or credible enough to students with low attendance. Instead, Aisha seeks turnaround role models: students who attend regularly now, but didn't previously. She identifies five, and trains them to be "support mentors." When a student's attendance slips, their first contact is with a support mentor, who discusses the barriers they face. Support mentors act as credible sources of guidance, while also reducing the burden on Aisha, and offering valuable suggestions and insights.

Step 3) Plan change

Aisha trains support mentors to help students make better plans. They plan when students should get up, what time they need an alarm, and alternatives if, for example, the bus is late. Support mentors follow up on key actions: for the first few days after meeting a student, they message to check they are following the plan; that they caught the bus on time, for example. Students record their plans, and share them with Aisha – this allows her to identify any unmet needs, and to pass the plans on to students' families, asking for their support.

Step 4) Initiate action

Aisha tries to make returning to school as easy as possible for students. When a student returns after a few days' absence, they start in her office, where they get breakfast and discuss what they've missed and how they can catch up. Aisha sets defaults, based around the number of days absent: if students are late or absent for more than three days in a term, they meet support mentors, after another two days, they meet her. She avoids publicising these triggers however: she doesn't want to suggest that absence is expected, or common.

Step 5) Follow up

Aisha monitors attendance closely, giving students daily feedback: on an attendance whiteboard outside her office, she records whether each class's attendance that day is above, at, or below the year group average (this indicates whether they will be eligible for the end-of-term attendance prize). A daily average (rather than an annual one) means students can improve their score overnight. (If a student has a justified absence, she excludes them from her calculations: this means social pressure is focused on students who should be in, not those who have a reason not to be.)

Aisha tries to make students feel they belong at school. Individually, if she knows who an absent student's close friends are, Aisha encourages them to message to check they are OK, and tell them they are being missed. If a student falls too far behind, she knows it's hard for them to catch up: when they do return to school, they are offered a fresh start, and their form makes a special effort to welcome them.

Aisha also tracks the effect of her approaches (whether attendance improves after a meeting with a support mentor, for example), and presents what she is learning to staff. This helps her to identify what's working, and refine her approach. For example, she finds better ways to help support mentors stay in touch with individual students, and to pass on their concerns.

Conclusion

Aisha's time remains limited, and she wishes she could get more support from other agencies. But the simple steps she asks teachers to take, and the social support mentors offer, help students feel that they belong in school. For a few students, mentors' help planning the details of getting to school on time makes a substantial difference. Making school seem more appealing, offering greater support, and planning how to arrive on time, helps increase the attendance of many of the students about whom Aisha had worried most.

6 How can we help students to stop?

Specify what students should stop doing

Discourage undesirable choices

Disrupt undesirable habits

Chapter map: how can we help students to stop?

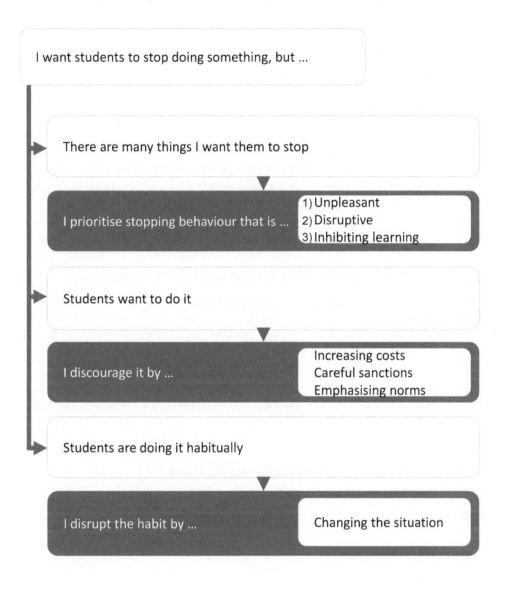

I want students to stop doing something, but …

There are many things I want them to stop

I prioritise stopping behaviour that is …
1) Unpleasant
2) Disruptive
3) Inhibiting learning

Students want to do it

I discourage it by …
Increasing costs
Careful sanctions
Emphasising norms

Students are doing it habitually

I disrupt the habit by …
Changing the situation

I promote desired behaviour alongside this (Chapters 1-5)

Copyright material from Harry Fletcher-Wood (2022), *Habits of Success: Getting Every Student Learning*, Routledge

The problem

This book has focused, so far, on how to help students adopt desirable behaviours – on getting them learning. Sometimes however, we need students to stop doing things, like making rude comments, running in corridors and cheating in tests. For example:

- Ray often burst out laughing in Diane's lessons
- Marco's students held themselves to unreasonably high standards.

Getting students to stop won't get them learning (Ray needs to focus more, not just laugh less). But focusing solely on what students should be doing won't prevent disruptive and dangerous behaviour: we need ways to stop students doing things too.

The principle: discourage and disrupt undesirable behaviours

We can help students to stop by discouraging undesirable choices, and by disrupting undesirable habits.

These strategies could be used in isolation, but we can also combine them with strategies from preceding chapters, in order both to discourage undesirable behaviour and to encourage habits of success.

6.1 If students are doing many undesirable things

Students usually know what they shouldn't be doing, but it's helpful to remove any ambiguity – and to focus our efforts. We can prioritise behaviours which:

1) Are unpleasant for others
2) Disrupt others' learning
3) Inhibit the student's own learning.

For example, we would prioritise rude comments above shouting out, and shouting out above doodling. Our priority may not be the most obvious issue: we may forestall arguments between students by preventing whispered comments, for example. Having chosen a priority, we can put it in concrete terms: "I'd like you to stop shouting out" is clearer than "I'd like you stop disrupting the lesson" (and is harder for students to resent, or dispute).

Specify the most important thing students should stop doing

Applications

- Ray often bursts our laughing: stopping this is a specific change, but Diane may identify and prioritise an underlying cause; Ray may be confused, or his peers may be making him laugh.
- Marco wanted his students to be less perfectionist: this is a broad aim; he may prioritise things students do which promote perfectionism, such as comparing their marks, or reviewing past work seeking errors.

Key idea

We can prioritise among the things we want students to stop by establishing:

- **Which behaviours are having the greatest negative impact on the class?**
- **What is causing the behaviour we want to stop?**

We can then discourage students from the action we want them to stop.

6.2 If students want to do something undesirable

Students must find their existing behaviour attractive or rewarding in some way. Even apparently purposeless behaviour has a motive: a student may be doodling to avoid boredom, or disrupting the lesson to show off. To understand their motive, we must get beyond ritualised conversations in which they assure us they'll do better; a question like "You must have had a reason . . . what was it?" may elicit an honest response, like "I thought it would be funny." Once we understand a student's motive, we can try to persuade them the action isn't worthwhile, either because it doesn't achieve their goal, or because the costs outweigh the benefits. We often given reasons - "distracting others means you're not learning, and nor are they" - but if these prove insufficient, we can make the costs of students' actions seem greater, and highlight role models and social norms which encourage change.

> *Show students their actions aren't worthwhile*

We can make the consequences feel more immediate

Poor behaviour has consequences - but some students seem not to consider them, or not to care. People generally don't calculate the costs and benefits of an action (and the chances of getting caught) before deciding what to do.[269] If the consequences are to influence students' decisions, therefore, we must highlight them before students act. For example, as students begin assessing each other's work, we might remind them that "Saying something unkind might seem funny now, but it won't when you're writing your apology letter later." Moreover, as we saw in Chapter 2, people care more about immediate costs and benefits than delayed ones. So an immediate sanction may influence students more than a delayed one (even if this means the sanction is weaker): better to ask students to move seats now, or to stay in at break, than to come back at the end of the day, or week. If we can't make the sanction immediate (we can't keep students in at break, for example), we can try to make it feel more immediate: "Take a second to consider where you'd like to be at the end of the day . . . I'm sure you'd rather not be back here." We can discourage actions by ensuring that the consequences are immediate, and that students consider them.

> *Make the consequences immediate, and ensure students consider them*

We can use sanctions to prompt change

A sanction can prompt students to change: some students receive one or two detentions early in the school year – and no more for the rest of the year.[270] Sometimes however, giving sanctions creates conflict, as students deny their actions, are uncertain what they've done, or feel unfairly treated. We can avoid conflict while giving sanctions by:

1)   Describing the reason: "You're calling out again, we'll discuss this after the lesson."
2)   Saying what students should be doing: "Put your hand up to contribute."
3)   Encouraging students to bounce back: "I'm looking forward to hearing your point."[271]

A rote punishment, like sitting in silence, is neither a powerful deterrent nor a good way to encourage change. A sanction need not be unpleasant – losing free time is a punishment in itself – but it should prompt students to rethink and amend their behaviour. For example, we can ask:

- Why are you here?
- Why was your action problematic?
- What are you going to do next?[272]

This helps us to understand their thinking (and the support they need), and to plan how they can avoid repeating the action (using strategies from preceding chapters). Helping students plan what to do if they are in the same situation again may help:[273] "If I'm tempted to shout out, I won't, I'll write my idea on my whiteboard instead." Sanctions can prompt students to change, if we give them carefully, and use them to review students' actions and plan alternatives.

> *Give sanctions carefully; use them to encourage change*

We can highlight role models

We discussed using role models to encourage desirable actions in Chapter 2; to use them to discourage undesirable actions, we must consider three additional things. First, recalling that students prefer role models who seem similar in some way, a role model who stopped doing something may be more compelling than one who never started: I tell struggling Year 11s about past students who turned themselves around, for example, not those who sailed through. Second, people can be influenced by negative role models – examples to avoid[274] – but we must introduce them cautiously. For example, if we describe a student who "kept doing what you're doing, and ultimately failed their exams," the listener may resent the comparison, or claim they're happy to fail. Instead, we could describe examples to avoid, but leave the comparison and implications implicit: "I'd like to tell you about a student I taught a few years ago . . ." Finally, we must consider what to do if a student is following a peer's poor example. We cannot criticise the peer, but we could highlight the sanctions they face, or reduce contact between them. Role models show that change is possible – and desirable – but only if students recognise and accept the comparison.

> *Role models can discourage action – if students accept them as role models*

We can highlight social norms

Social norms can discourage undesirable behaviour. We can use the strategies described in Chapter 2, emphasising that desirable behaviour is prevalent – "Almost everyone is putting their hand up" – or increasing: "More and more of us are getting this right." If their friends are behaving poorly however, students may ignore prevalent good behaviour: people are more influenced by their perceived peers than by the whole group.[275] Since undesirable social norms influence people too,[276] we should avoid calling attention to poor behaviour (if possible), either by challenging it privately or, if a public challenge is necessary, by emphasising what should happen, not what's wrong: "I'm waiting for everyone to begin," rather than "I can see two people still talking." Finally, sanctions emphasise and enforce expected behaviour. When students saw a peer cheat with impunity, cheating doubled,[277] so even though some students don't change in response to sanctions (they need help changing their habits, discussed below),[278] sanctioning their behaviour still matters, because it conveys what's expected and accepted *to the rest of the community*: "What Jenny said to Abdul was unacceptable: she'll be in detention at the end of the day."

> *Ensure students know that most of their peers are behaving well*

Applications

- Ray often bursts out laughing: if Diane thinks this is intentional, she may emphasise that the rest of the class are focusing, or give an immediate sanction. Alternatively, if she feels that Ray's response isn't under his control, she may examine what's prompting it more closely (we discuss this in the next section).
- Marco wanted his students to be less perfectionist: he could ask an older student to describe learning to worry less about this, or he could highlight the immediate benefit of accepting a piece of work is finished – students can stop thinking about it.

Key idea

We can discourage students from making undesirable choices by asking ourselves:

- **How can I ensure the immediate costs seem greater than the immediate benefits?**
- **How can sanctions encourage change?**
- **What role models will encourage students to stop?**
- **How can I show that prevalent behaviour is positive, and that expected behaviour matters?**

These strategies should discourage undesirable decisions, but they won't stop undesirable habits. For example, sanctions help: detentions improved some students' behaviour. But a quarter of students received more and more detentions across the year: the cost of their behaviour grew, but this didn't influence their actions.[279] Similarly, some teenagers were able to stop smoking by planning what to do when tempted – but this didn't help those with a strong smoking habit.[280] Motivating students to stop still matters (students must work with us if they are to change), but we may rely on motivation too much. If students are struggling to stop, we must tackle their habits.[281]

> *If students are acting habitually, we need to change their habits, not just their intentions*

6.3 If students are acting habitually

Stopping an existing habit is hard. A person initiates a habit because they have a goal: when he gets stuck with his homework, Michael wants a break, so he checks his phone. If Michael does this enough times, it becomes a habit: whenever he gets stuck, he checks his phone (the situation – getting stuck – has come to prompt the action, as we discussed in Chapter 5). Changing habits is hard because getting stuck will continue to prompt him to check his phone – even if his goal changes, and he wants to focus better.[282] So the key to overcoming a habit isn't motivation or willpower – it's breaking the link between the situation and the habit:[283] Michael should work somewhere different, or leave his phone in another room, rather than trying to ignore its presence. We can help students change their habits by changing the situations prompting them.

> *Motivation may not be enough to change a habit: we need to break the link between the situation and the habit*

We can change the situation

We can disrupt an undesirable habit by identifying and changing the situation which prompts it. We often identify social situations causing undesirable behaviour: we change the seating plan to separate students who distract each other, for example. We need to look at events in the same way, asking ourselves "What's prompting this habit?" We could mentally replay the lesson, invite a colleague to observe, or ask students directly, "What starts you off?" Having identified the prompt, we can reshape the situation: if getting stuck is prompting students to give up on independent tasks, for example, we could pause to review the model after they've started (but before they get stuck). Similarly, if students lose focus when moving from the carpet to their tables, we could send them in small groups, time how long they take to settle, or explain the next task first - anything which makes the situation feel different. Changes to our room, group, or lesson routine are also opportunities to change prompts. For example, if discussions often get out of hand, we can use a set change to introduce new ways to begin them ("Write your ideas silently first"), and alternatives to interrupting ("Write ideas on your whiteboard if it's not your turn"). Finally, students can use this approach too: if they frequently lose focus when doing homework in their room, they can try doing it at school, or with a parent. Identifying and changing prompts disrupts undesirable habits.

> *Identify and change what's prompting the undesirable habit*

We can make the action harder

Adding "friction" - a barrier to action - disrupts an undesirable habit.[284] A person putting their chocolate on a high shelf is creating friction: they're hoping to change their behaviour, by making reaching it a little harder. Such changes may seem trivial, but they matter: reducing how much paracetamol people can buy created a small barrier (people can just go to two shops) - but it halved deaths from paracetamol poisoning, by reducing how much people have at home.[285] We can create friction through procedures and delay: if too many students are wandering around the classroom, we could tell students to "Ask me before getting up" (a procedure) or to "Wait until everyone else is sitting down" (a delay). Friction can also encourage productive habits: if students call out answers, we could ask them to write their answer before raising their hand; this disrupts the habit, and gets all students thinking. Students can add friction themselves: they can make getting side-tracked from homework harder, for example, by putting their phone in another room, or giving it to a parent until they've finished. Delays and procedures disrupt undesirable habits, and - by making students pause - encourage them to consider what they really want to do.

> *Create friction by adding delays and procedures which make undesirable habits harder*

Applications

- Ray laughed uncontrollably: Diane can identify prompts for his laughter - such as peers' actions, or things she says - and try to change them.
- Marco wanted his students to be less perfectionist: he could identify and change situations which promote this; for example, he could make it harder for students to compare their work by returning it without a grade, or by returning it individually while students are working silently.

> ## Key idea
>
> **We can help students to break undesirable habits by asking:**
>
> - **What situation prompts the habit? How can I change it?**
> - **How can I make the undesirable behaviour harder?**

We can combine these strategies with those suggested in Chapter 4, so we are both disrupting the undesirable habit and encouraging a better alternative, by making it easier, and practising whenever students slip.

Conclusion

We can help students to stop doing something by asking:

- What, exactly, do I want students to stop doing?
- How can I discourage them from doing it?

And, if the action is habitual:

- How can I disrupt the habit?

Persistence should reward us: giving detentions, and ensuring students attended, meant Laura McInerney "needed to give them out a lot less."[286] As we monitor the impact of our efforts, we may identify other motives and prompts for students' behaviour: we can keep relaunching the change, modifying what we say, and the support we offer, until it works. Finally, we can help students to recognise their improvements, and what they signify, using the strategies described in Chapter 5: highlighting what we notice - "You contributed so many good points in the lesson today" - and asking students to recognise what this says about them: "What are you proud of doing differently this term?"

✓ Checklist

I help students to stop	
1) If students are doing many undesirable things, I . . .	
• Specify the most important change	*I want students to stop making rude comments about each other's answers.*
2) If students want to do something undesirable, I . . .	
• Make the consequences feel more immediate	*"If you do that again, I'll ask you to move seats."*
• Use sanctions to prompt change	*"Write what you did, why it's a problem, and what you'll do differently next time."*
• Offer role models of change	*"I had a student two years ago who really struggled to focus, but then . . ."*
• Emphasise social norms	*"Almost everyone has started writing."*
3) If students are acting habitually, I . . .	
• Change the situation	*Stopping students and asking them to review the model before they lose focus.*
• Make the action harder	*"Please check with me before standing up."*
I monitor the results and refine my approach until students sustain the change, while helping them to recognise that they're changing.	

Copyright material from Harry Fletcher-Wood (2022), *Habits of Success: Getting Every Student Learning*, Routledge

Workshop 6: getting Liam to stop challenging teachers

What's the situation?

For the first time in several years, Mike has been given a new Year 7 form. A few weeks into term, he has become concerned about Liam's behaviour. He seems to be struggling with the reduced oversight and personal contact which secondary school offers: he's not doing much work; instead, he's challenging teachers and distracting peers. Mike has seen students form poor habits in Year 7, then struggle to break them. What can he do to disrupt Liam's developing bad habits, and to help him build better ones? (This is a situation which I suspect most Year 7 tutors have experienced.)

What would you suggest?

1)   What - precisely - should the student stop?
2)   How would you discourage the student from doing it?
3)   How would you disrupt the undesirable habit?

Step 1) Specify the change

Mike first seeks to clarify the challenge. He asks all colleagues to send him one line on any concerns they have about Liam's behaviour, and another line on any successes. He reviews this, alongside the information from Liam's primary school. Challenging teachers appears to be a consistent concern, possibly as a way of covering up Liam's confusion about what he should be doing. Mike prioritises stopping Liam from challenging teachers - because this is likely to cause him serious problems, and sets a poor example for the class - alongside building a new habit of asking for help.

Step 2) Discourage undesirable behaviour

Mike takes three steps to encourage Liam to change. First, he sets an immediate consequence: any email or record on the school's systems of challenging a teacher will lead to a detention the same day. Second, he asks a student from his old form, now in Year 12, to describe how challenging teachers in Years 7 and 8 brought negligible benefits and substantial costs. Finally, he discusses the problem Liam faces - not understanding what he's being asked to do - and tries to show Liam that asking for help addresses the problem and will offer immediate reassurance.

Step 3) Disrupt undesirable habits

Mike shares his findings with colleagues in a brief email. He highlights the situation which appears to be causing the problem: "When Liam is unsure what to do, he can be disruptive: he sometimes challenges teachers, rather than admit he is struggling." Mike tactfully suggests a way to avoid it: "If you are able to check with Liam when students are starting independent work, this may help." He also tries to make it easier for Liam to ask for help. He plans sentence starters, such as "Excuse me sir/miss, could you just explain ____ again," practises them with Liam, and has him write them on the front of his planner as a reminder.

Conclusion

Mike checks on Liam's progress, asking teachers for a one-line update two and four weeks later; he uses these to consider whether Liam needs additional support. He tries to visit his form during a lesson every week, during which he checks whether Liam is asking for help, and whether his planner is on his desk as a reminder. He ensures Liam recognises the progress he's making, and encourages him to see himself as a student who knows what's going on, checks if he's unsure, and gets on with teachers. The effort Mike makes on this one change is substantial – but he believes that getting it right now is crucial, and should transform Liam's experience of school.

7 How can we encourage teachers to change?

Specify the change: pick a priority, then choose a powerful habit or small step to achieve it

Inspire and motivate teachers to value the change

PLan change: ask teachers to commit to action

Initiate action: make starting easy

Follow up: help teachers keep going

Chapter map: how can we encourage teachers to change?

Change is particularly hard for teachers:
- They have strong habits
- They are attached to existing practice
- They can easily avoid change

Teachers will welcome autonomy – but we must remain faithful to the strategy

If there are many things to change

| Specify the change | Pick the priority | Encourage a habit |
| | | Set a bitesize goal |

If teachers aren't convinced the change is worthwhile

Inspire and motivate	Explain why; help teachers make it their own
	Minimise immediate costs and highlight benefits
	Show teachers their peers are changing

If teachers mean to act, then forget

| Plan change | Ask teachers to commit |
| | Help them recall commitments |

If teachers struggle to start

| Make starting easy | Set productive defaults |
| | Practise |

If teachers start, then stop

| Follow up | Highlight progress |
| | Relaunch the habit |

Copyright material from Harry Fletcher-Wood (2022), *Habits of Success: Getting Every Student Learning*, Routledge

We want teachers to change too. School leaders create policies, teacher educators plan professional development, teachers ask their colleagues for help. But change is hard for teachers, just as it is for students. Like students, teachers' responses range from enthusiastic to sceptical. Like students, teachers forget things and get side-tracked; unlike students, teachers are extremely busy. Policies may be overlooked, professional development ideas forgotten, requests missed. Two things make change particularly hard: teachers' existing habits, and their preferences.

Change is hard for teachers too

School life encourages teachers to form habits: this makes change harder. People form habits when they repeat an action in a specific situation: teachers repeat some actions many times each day; how they settle students and address disruption soon becomes a habit.[287] These habits are individual – Ms Shah always begins by reviewing the previous lesson – and organisational: teachers always line students up before a lesson. Habits let teachers focus on students' learning (rather than entry routines),[288] and ensure that students and teachers know "exactly what to expect of one another" – but they may remain unchanged for decades.[289] This seems counter-intuitive: schools respond continually to new initiatives, curricula and inspection frameworks; but these affect documents, policies and job titles more than they do teachers' and students' classroom activity.[290] Habits help teachers to teach effectively, but they make change harder.

Habits make teaching easier, but make change harder

Teachers can avoid change, and often have good reason to do so. Even an enthusiastic teacher will struggle to change without sufficient time, support and resources.[291] But teachers may not be enthusiastic: they have adopted practices which seem to work; change means neglecting them (and re-evaluating past efforts) in favour of unfamiliar and unproven alternatives. Experiencing failed initiatives further saps enthusiasm for change.[292] Moreover, teachers retain substantial autonomy: most lessons go unobserved, most decisions go unnoticed, unrecorded and unremarked. So an unenthusiastic teacher can resist change subtly, effectively (perhaps unintentionally), by politely prioritising something else. Teachers will only change if we can convince them that doing so is manageable, and worthwhile.

We must convince teachers the change is manageable, and worthwhile

This chapter shows how strategies drawn from behavioural science, and described in previous chapters, can be used to encourage teachers to act, whether we are creating a whole-school policy or arranging a room swap. I've offered evidence and examples specific to working with teachers (but have not repeated evidence discussed previously). These strategies can be pursued in many ways: a specific plan makes change more likely, for example, but the details could be set by the head, agreed by a department, or decided by a teacher. Newer (and struggling) teachers are likely to benefit from more direction; more experienced and effective teachers from greater autonomy. The more control teachers have, the more they are likely to welcome (and sustain) change – but we must balance this autonomy with fidelity to the strategy we're pursuing; anyone can make the plan, but it must be specific.

> *Teachers will welcome autonomy – but we must also remain faithful to the strategy*

7.1 What should we ask teachers to change?

If there are many things to change

Once, I tried to change two things at once: I asked different questions and paused longer between student responses. This absorbed all my attention and undermined my classroom routines, derailing lessons: it taught me to change one thing at a time. It's unrealistic to expect teachers to make several meaningful changes at once – to act on several items of feedback, for example. Yet it's tempting: one senior leader described how, when she was first promoted, she was "constantly trying to change everything as I felt this would have an impact and in any new job you want to prove you have done something." Instead, we must help teachers to focus on the change most likely to increase students' learning,[293] by choosing an aspect of teaching, identifying the fundamental challenge teachers face, and allowing them to focus on it.

1) Choose an aspect of teaching

Prioritising may seem difficult when there are so many things teachers must do well (and when we wish to avoid jumping to conclusions). We can begin by choosing an aspect of teaching to consider, based on the school's current goals, strengths, and challenges. (We might choose one priority for the whole school, or specific priorities for departments or individuals; as I suggested above, this choice, and subsequent ones, can be made by, with or for teachers.) We could choose between the persistent challenges all teachers face:

- Planning learning
- Assessing students' understanding
- Enlisting students' participation
- Managing classroom behaviour.[294]

Or, if our school has articulated principles of learning, we could choose between them; at Mossbourne Academy, for example, these include:

- Behaviour and routines
- Explanation and modelling
- Scaffold and challenge.[295]

Having chosen the aspect of teaching we most want to improve, we can examine current practice within it more closely, to identify the fundamental challenge teachers currently face.

> *Choose a broad aspect of teaching to focus upon*

2) Identify the fundamental challenge

The challenges teachers face must be addressed in order. A teacher cannot design efficient checks for understanding unless they have set precise learning goals; they cannot get students to commit to a plan until they have motivated them to act. This means we must prioritise the most fundamental challenge – the first – with which teachers are struggling. We can identify it by taking a sequence of steps towards success (within the aspect of teaching we have chosen), and examining how well teachers are managing each step, talking to them, observing lessons, and reviewing student work. To improve students' participation and behaviour, we can use the sequence suggested by Chapters 1 to 5, supporting teachers to:

1) Specify the change
2) Inspire and motivate students to value it
3) Help students commit to a plan
4) Make starting easy
5) Help students keep going.

(As we discussed in Chapter 1, the change teachers specify for their students should address the most fundamental challenge *students* face: focusing, applying appropriate techniques, persevering and contributing.) To improve planning and assessment, we can use the sequence suggested in my previous book, *Responsive Teaching*,[296] supporting teachers to:

1) Choose what to teach, in the limited time they have
2) Show students what success looks like
3) Check what students have understood in a lesson
4) Identify what students are thinking during a lesson
5) Help students improve.

Alternatively, we could break down improvement in the subject or phase into a sequence of steps. The first step with which teachers are struggling – the most fundamental challenge – is our priority.

> *Identify the fundamental challenge*

3) Help teachers focus on the priority

Prioritising is hard. Saying "This matters" is easy; saying "This matters more than my other tasks" is harder; neglecting those other tasks is harder still. Teachers may feel tempted – or obliged – to take on new tasks while continuing everything they are doing already. This makes change unsustainable, and workload unmanageable. We must license, encourage and support them to drop less important tasks, in order to overcome the fundamental challenge. We can:

- Show that one task replaces another: "Trying whole-class feedback will mean marking books less often."
- Ask teachers to stop doing things: "To create time for this, we'd like to cut after-school interventions."
- Ask teachers to identify less important activities they can stop.

Unless the priority is clear – and unless we emphasise that prioritising means favouring some tasks and neglecting others – we risk overwhelming teachers and undermining their attempts to change: we must help teachers focus on the priority (and manage their workload) by explicitly deprioritising other tasks.

> *Help teachers focus on the priority by deprioritising other tasks*

If we want teachers to make a lasting change

For a change to last, it must become a habit. Teachers are under continual pressure to change: if a change doesn't become a habit, something new will take its place.[297] This means we must take the challenge we have prioritised, and identify a habit which addresses it. Debbie Light, Vice Principal at Ark Acton Academy, applied this approach to the school's teaching and learning policy. She transformed principles, like "Connect to previous lessons' key knowledge and skills," into habits, like "Begin every lesson with a silent 5-a-day retrieval practice that requires students to recall knowledge from current and previous topics." (At the time, the school was in special measures; elsewhere, she might have been less prescriptive.) The principle is excellent – but excellent principles and carefully written policies don't create lasting change. A habit helps teachers apply the principle consistently – habits are the key to lasting change.

> *For a change to last, it must become a habit*

Since change is hard for teachers, and forming new habits takes time, the habits we encourage must be powerful. Powerful habits are simple enough to stick, and fertile enough to make a difference (as we discussed in Chapter 1). For example, using exit tickets is simple: it's frequent (every lesson), concrete (a short individual task), and rapid (taking five minutes, and showing what students have understood immediately). It's also fertile: it's flexible (an exit ticket can take many forms), promotes wider change (by encouraging teachers to set clear objectives, and respond to what students have understood), and supports collaboration (teachers can compare what students have understood, and ways to respond).[298] Josh

Goodrich, at Oasis South Bank, wanted teachers to plan better questions: the options he considered illustrate the design of a powerful habit. He thought about:

- Asking teachers to script questions – but this wouldn't ensure they timed questions well, or responded effectively.
- Asking teachers to identify students' misconceptions – this would give teachers flexibility about what to do, but what they learned wouldn't be obvious.
- Asking teachers to bring data on students' most common misconceptions to department meetings – this meant teachers planned and used their questions (and could get help from colleagues if they had struggled); it also encouraged teachers to compare what they had learned, and discuss how best to respond.

So the powerful habit became: "Identify the most common student misconception in one lesson each week; bring what you learn to the department meeting." Powerful habits can be used to promote anything, from deeper subject knowledge (sharing recent reading in department meetings, for example), to wellbeing (asking teachers to name a colleague who has supported them each week). Powerful habits – simple and fertile – are the key to lasting improvement.

> *Identify a powerful habit - simple and fertile - which addresses the priority*

If we want teachers to make an immediate change

Sometimes we want teachers to change immediately – to address challenging classroom behaviour, for example. Teachers improve rapidly when bigger goals – like improving literacy, or getting students to focus – are broken into immediately achievable steps (and teachers are supported to pursue them).[299] For example, Elizabeth Mountstevens wanted to improve her chemistry students' literacy; she chose a bitesize first step (both for her, and for students): planning answers to longer questions on sticky notes.[300] Once we have chosen a fundamental challenge, we can break the changes needed to address it into a sequence of smaller goals. For example, improving planning can be broken into:

1) Identifying the key learning point from the lesson, then;
2) Designing an assessment that shows whether students have understood it, then;
3) Designing a practice task to master the key learning point.

If teachers struggle, we can break each step down further: identifying the key learning point becomes "Identify everything students should know at the end of the lesson," then "Identify what students should already know and what's new this lesson," for example. Bitesize goals help whatever we want teachers to do: it's easier for them to "Circulate around the classroom" than to "Pre-empt off-task behaviour"; it's easier for them to respond to an email with one clear request than to a list of issues and actions. To encourage immediate change, we must offer bitesize goals.

> *To encourage immediate change, offer bitesize goals*

Applications

- Charlotte was worried that teachers were using the school's behaviour management system too rigidly, giving sanctions automatically, rather than using the system to support their classroom management techniques. A powerful habit might be for Charlotte to review sanctions daily with heads of year: this could reveal which students and teachers need more support. A bitesize goal for teachers could be trying one more positive technique – such as emphasising desirable social norms – before issuing a sanction.
- Mark wanted experienced colleagues to engage with research and experiment with new teaching approaches. Bitesize goals could make this feel less risky: he could ask them to read a single paper or blog post, or attend a single reading discussion, hoping that this piques their curiosity. He could then invite them to try a small change based on what they have read.
- Jeanette needed Ali (one of her senior leaders) to manage his time and tasks more effectively. She could meet Ali on Fridays, reviewing what he had achieved that week (and any barriers he had encountered), and planning what to do (and when) the following week.

Key idea

To decide what to change, we can ask:

- **What aspect of teaching do we most need to improve? What is the first step with which teachers are struggling – the fundamental challenge?**
- **What powerful habit – simple and fertile – would make a lasting difference? Or:**
- **What bitesize goal would permit immediate improvement?**
- **How can I help teachers prioritise this (and deprioritise other tasks)?**

Teachers are likely to find change more attractive if they have a clear goal (or a simple habit) to pursue, and if they are encouraged to prioritise it over other tasks. But we will still need to convince them that the change is worthwhile.

7.2 How can we convince teachers to change?

When we introduce a change, we've already persuaded ourselves it's worthwhile, through reading and training, seeing it and trying it. Unless our colleagues have shared these experiences, they won't share our belief – convinced ourselves, we may underestimate the need to convince them. This section discusses three reasons teachers may be sceptical, and strategies to address them.

If teachers don't see the value of the change . . .

We can demonstrate the rationale

When teachers see that a change will help them better meet students' needs, they adopt it willingly.[301] To show that this is the case, we could offer evidence, citing specific studies, or summaries, such as the EEF Toolkit. We might also appeal to principles – "Students need feedback to improve" – or authorities: "Dylan Wiliam says that 'feedback should be more work for the recipient than the donor.'" Teachers may suspect a change is a fad: introducing the "forgetting curve" (illustrating how fast people forget new information), I explain that it was first described in 1885, and was replicated in 2015; its validity and value has endured. Finally, seeing the impact of a change can be compelling: nurses found a task particularly motivating when they met someone whose life it had saved, for example.[302] We could share students' accounts of how the change has helped them, or connect it to teachers' experiences, as teachers or as learners. Demonstrating the rationale for change begins to show its value.

> *Demonstrate the rationale for change*

We can link the change to a challenge

Describing the rationale may help, but many change initiatives fail because they tell teachers what they need, rather than "attending to what teachers demand."[303] Many of these demands are predictable: all teachers want their students to succeed, and want to go home at a reasonable time. The challenges are predictable too: it's hard to get all students focused, and to make complicated ideas comprehensible.[304] So, rather than beginning by describing the change and its rationale, we could begin by exploring the challenge it addresses. For example, we could ask teachers:

- "When did students' focus last slip?"
- "When did students last forget something they should have known?"
- "How many students are doing their homework regularly?"

Starting with the challenge frames the change as a way to reduce teachers' burdens, not add to them: a new routine should help students focus; retrieval practice should reduce forgetting. Moreover, discussing the challenge allows us to advocate change without implying criticism – change is needed because teaching is hard, not because you're teaching badly – and to forestall the suggestion that everything is going perfectly, and no change is needed.

> *Discuss the challenge before introducing the change*

We can help teachers make the change their own

Finally, change is likely to be more motivating, and more effective, if teachers make it their own: we can encourage them to identify what their students need, and to tailor the change to suit them. Seeing their existing practice in a new light motivates teachers to change:[305] realising I was overlooking student misconceptions inspired me to adapt my questioning. We can encourage such realisations by asking teachers to review students' work with colleagues: this helps them to identify gaps in students' understanding, and ways to address them.[306] Moreover, teachers are more likely to change if they can choose how to achieve a goal than if they are told exactly what to do.[307] Instead of mandating exit tickets, we can agree a goal – "knowing what students understand at the end of each lesson" – examine different ways to achieve it (including exit tickets), and help teachers develop one which suits them. (Whatever teachers choose, it must achieve the goal: verbal questioning alone won't capture what every student understands, for example.) Change will be more motivating if teachers recognise its value to their students, and tailor it to their needs.

> *Help teachers identify their students' needs, and tailor the change to meet them*

If teachers don't think the effort is worthwhile

We can minimise the cost of change

The strategies described so far may convince teachers that change is a good idea – but they must also believe it's worth the effort required. Often, we ask teachers to make rapid and significant changes, but these demand time and effort, and disrupt existing routines. We can minimise these costs by limiting how much we ask teachers to change at once. For example, if we want teachers to stop marking individual books entirely (and give whole-class feedback instead), we can ask them to begin by marking one class's books one less time a week (rather than stopping entirely with all their classes). We could emphasise that time spent on the change is not an additional cost, but one which would have been incurred at some point anyway: "Planning questions for the scheme of work will take time – but if we don't do it, we'll have to plan them each lesson anyway." Finally, if costs are unavoidable, we can acknowledge them, emphasise we have minimised them, and offset them against other tasks: "I know this will take time, I've made it as quick as possible, and we'll cancel this week's briefing to help compensate." Minimising costs helps make a desirable change seem worthwhile.

> *Minimise the cost of change*

We can highlight the benefits of change

We can also make a change seem worthwhile by framing the benefits in tempting ways. For example, almost all teachers agree they have "more to learn," but only two thirds believe they have "weaknesses in their instruction":[308] we may want to frame changes as a chance to learn – not a way to address weaknesses. A recruitment message seeking those who "thrive in challenging environments" proved twice as attractive to early-career teachers as one seeking those "committed to improving the lives of children."[309] Everything we do should improve children's lives: we may make a change (or a job) seem more worthwhile by showing that it also offers new challenges and opportunities: "This should help students, and teach us to use a cutting-edge technology." If people see a change as risky, highlighting the cost of not changing can prove compelling (as we discussed in Chapter 2): we might emphasise that "Current practice is brilliant, but I worry it's not sustainable." Finally, positive effects are the best evidence a change is working: having started, we can ask teachers what benefits they have noticed. Highlighting tempting benefits helps make change seem worthwhile.

> *Highlight benefits which tempt teachers*

If teachers don't accept the change

We can show that their peers are changing

Role models and social norms encourage change (as we discussed in Chapter 2). For example, the role models new teachers encounter influence the teachers they wish to become.[310] People choose their own role models,[311] and measure themselves against others who seem similar (for example, other maths teachers).[312] We can introduce teachers to multiple potential role models: encouraging new teachers to observe a different colleague each week; asking teachers from several departments to present their experiences of a change. From this range of colleagues, teachers can then identify the role models with whom they most associate. (Introducing multiple examples also shows that the change is viable – if maths, English and geography have all tried it, it probably works – and implies a social norm.) We can highlight positive norms – "Almost everyone managed to do a peer observation last week" – while challenging undesirable ones privately: emailing specific colleagues takes longer, but it's better than conveying an undesirable norm by telling all staff that "over thirty registers still aren't done from Period 1." If teachers know their peers are changing, they will change too.

> *Show teachers their peers are changing*

Applications

- Charlotte wanted teachers to use the school's behaviour management system in a more nuanced way. She could ask them about challenges which applying the system rigidly has created – students becoming increasingly oppositional, for example – and invite them to describe ways they have applied it firmly but flexibly.
- Mark wanted experienced colleagues to engage with research, and experiment with new teaching approaches. He could ask about the challenges they face

currently, and offer research or suggest teaching strategies to address them. He might also invite teachers who have been reading research with him to explain how they've used it, and the benefits they've seen. (By setting a bitesize goal – read one paper – he has already minimised the cost of starting.)

- Jeanette needed Ali (one of her senior leaders) to manage his time and tasks more effectively: she could discuss the challenges with him, then ask him to find out how other senior leaders manage their time.

Key idea

Teachers will only try a change if it seems worthwhile. We can ask ourselves:

- How can I help teachers recognise the value of the change?
- How can I ensure the benefits justify the costs?
- How can I show that other teachers are changing?

If our priority and goal are appropriate, these strategies should help. If colleagues object however, (particularly if they object having given the change a chance) we may need to reconsider and refine the goal with them, until we can agree on its value.

Teachers may be convinced the change matters, but the pressures they are under may mean they struggle to act on their intentions: if so, we can encourage them to commit to a plan.

7.3 How can we help teachers to commit to action?

If teachers mean to act, then forget . . .

We can ask teachers to commit to a plan

Sometimes we discuss what to change, but not when and how – we leave teachers to choose a time (and prepare) later. But teachers may intend to act, then find more urgent tasks get in the way. Committing to a plan helps people fulfil their intentions (as we discussed in Chapter 3). We can ask teachers to specify when they will act: "I'll highlight positive social norms in my next Year 9 lesson." They may need to choose a point in the lesson too, deciding whether to address a misconception before or after students encounter it, for example. Making a plan may reveal other adaptations required for the change to work – to elicit the misconception, teachers might need to ask a specific question. (Practising the change, discussed below, helps teachers test and refine their plans further: it could show teachers they need to prepare for students' follow-up questions about the misconception, for example.) Committing to a plan prepares teachers to act.

> *Ask teachers to commit to a plan*

We can help teachers to recall and prioritise their plan

Having made a plan, we need to help teachers act on it: we can do so by asking them to commit to others, and set reminders. In two of the most effective forms of professional development (instructional coaching and teacher learning communities) teachers make explicit commitments to colleagues (either to their coach or their fellow teachers).[313] Teachers consistently report that this helps them prioritise action:[314] having been given time to pursue a professional development project for example, Elizabeth Mountstevens knew that she would need to have something to talk about in our discussion group: "this gives me the incentive I need."[315] Some teachers commit to their students, which both introduces the change, and helps them stick to it: "I plan to ask a question, pause, then nominate someone to respond, so everyone's thinking . . . please remind me if I forget." Finally, Freya Odell committed to improving her wellbeing by planning fun weekend activities: paying for these in advance meant she felt "committed to attending."[316] Reminders then help teachers stick to their plans. These could be implicit: in instructional coaching, the coach returns to see the intended change the following week; in teacher learning communities, teachers describe how the change went to their peers. Alternatively, teachers can set themselves reminders, on phones, planners or PowerPoints: one trainee used sticky notes around the room, such as a reminder of entry routines on the doorframe. (If students get used to the reminders teachers set for themselves, this may prompt them to act too.) Commitments and reminders help teachers recall and prioritise their plans.

> *Ask teachers to commit to others and to set reminders*

Applications

- Charlotte wanted teachers to use the school's behaviour management system in a more nuanced way. She could invite them to plan a response to a common but ambiguous situation, such as: "A student is distracting others, but you're not sure it's intentional . . ." She could then ask teachers to create reminders for themselves, by summarising the plan on a sticky note – "Unsure it's intentional: give a reminder initially" – and putting it on their computer or desk.
- Mark wanted experienced colleagues to engage with research, and experiment with new teaching approaches. Hopefully, discussing research will offer his colleagues some promising ideas: Mark could ask them to commit to trying one before the next discussion.
- Jeanette needed Ali (one of her senior leaders) to manage his time and tasks more effectively. She could help him to plan the best time for each of the following week's tasks, and ask him to set reminders, written or electronic, of his plans.

Key idea

If teachers mean to act, but find it hard to do so, we can identify ways to help by asking ourselves:

- How can I help teachers plan when and how to act?
- Who could teachers commit to?
- What would remind them of their commitments?

Having planned the change, we can make it easier for teachers to begin.

7.4 How can we encourage teachers to start?

If teachers aren't sure how to start . . .

We can set a default

Teachers may want to act, but may not be sure where to begin. If they want to introduce regular retrieval practice, for example, they must decide what to ask, when to ask, and what to do if students can't answer. They may lack time to set questions; they may choose times which don't work. As we discussed in Chapter 4, defaults make starting easier by resolving these decisions: we can suggest questions (on the scheme of work), times (the start of the lesson) and responses (give the correct answers, but only go into them if students hold significant misconceptions). Defaults aren't rules (teachers are free to choose better questions and times): they're guidance for those unsure how to begin. Whenever teachers are starting something new, we can identify crucial decisions (either by anticipating them, or from teachers' questions) and offer acceptable defaults: "If you're not sure how to start, it's usually fine to . . ." Conversely, if teachers are struggling to change, we may look for defaults which are hindering them: writing comments in students' books (the existing default) may be encouraging a teacher to write too much; comments on sticky notes (a new default) could encourage concision. Defaults make starting easier, by clarifying how to begin.

Clarify how to begin by setting defaults

If teachers struggle to get started . . .

We can practise

Teachers are often invited to consider change: to discuss its merits, examine examples and (perhaps) plan action. Compared to other professionals however, teachers spend relatively little time practising – that is, practising teaching *outside* the classroom, in an environment in which they can try changes, and make mistakes and refinements.[317] Practising new techniques makes teachers much more likely to use them (compared to reflection alone):[318]

practice is a way to gain confidence and fluency in unfamiliar actions,[319] *before* trying them in the classroom. For example, in a professional development session about student misconceptions, we would certainly discuss likely misconceptions – but teachers could also plan how to respond, practise their responses with colleagues, and refine them using colleagues' feedback. Effective practice activities target specific, crucial aspects of teaching (just like effective priorities, as we discussed above):[320] if teachers want students to focus better, they could practise strategies like giving concise, concrete instructions, and highlighting social norms. As teachers succeed, we can make practice harder and more realistic: asking them to address a misconception while keeping a distracted student focused, for example. (That said, we want practice to help teachers form desirable habits: it should always be pitched to ensure they are succeeding.) Practising a change outside the classroom makes it easier for teachers to apply it inside the classroom.

> Let teachers practise a change outside the classroom, before they try it in the classroom

Applications

- Charlotte wanted teachers to use the school's behaviour management system in a more nuanced way. Teachers could practise strategies to pre-empt challenging behaviour, such as highlighting positive social norms.
- Mark wanted experienced colleagues to engage with research, and experiment with new teaching approaches. Practice could help them read research confidently: he could read a paper with colleagues, helping them to make sense of the technical terms, conventions and conclusions.
- Jeanette needed Ali (one of her senior leaders) to manage his time and tasks more effectively. Defaults could make prioritising easier for him: they could agree which tasks to do first, for example, and when he should ask for help.

Key idea

We can make starting easier by asking ourselves:

- **What defaults would clarify how to begin?**
- **Could teachers practise the change before trying it in the classroom?**

Once teachers have begun, we can help them maintain momentum.

7.5 How can we help teachers keep going?

Unless teachers turn the change into a habit, it will eventually slip, because something else will arise to absorb their time and attention.[321] People form a habit by repeating an action in a specific situation, as we discussed in Chapter 5. The plans and reminders teachers set can help them to do this: Elizabeth Mountstevens built a habit for herself (and her students) by always giving them sticky notes to plan extended answers.[322] But nascent habits are fragile: Joel Mendes described how breaks in routine for students broke his routines as well: "after half-term I was forgetting to do the new things that I had decided to try at the start of the term." We can encourage teachers to keep going by ensuring that the change feels worthwhile, and by helping them to restart if they stop.

If teachers don't feel it's worth continuing

We can highlight progress

Teachers may not feel they are making progress. Improvement can be slow, and teachers may focus on the challenges that remain, rather than their successes. If we are to highlight their progress (and adapt the change to ensure it works) we need to track what's changing, without creating an oppressive or onerous system. If we have chosen a powerful habit, progress should be obvious: if teachers are bringing student misconceptions to department meetings for example, no further monitoring is needed. For teachers pursuing bitesize goals, we can look for progress using our existing lesson visits or reviews of students' work. If we must create new ways to track progress, they should be simple and positive: for example, we could ask colleagues to share successes, such as the "most surprising misconception" or the "best example of dual coding" from the half term. Once we know what progress teachers are making, we can celebrate it.

> *Find simple, positive ways to track teachers' progress*

If teachers are to keep going, the change must feel worthwhile. Researchers have tried offering teachers money to improve student performance, but have achieved negligible benefits at substantial cost (while raising ethical questions).[323] Teachers may welcome token rewards – cards, bottles, chocolates – particularly if these are unexpected, and recognise specific actions, as we discussed in Chapter 5. Simple gestures go a long way too: teachers say they want more private, "genuine recognition" from line managers,[324] and one experiment found they particularly appreciated an email which simply said, "Thank you for all of your hard work."[325] Most powerful however, may be helping teachers to recognise the intrinsic value of their efforts. People are particularly motivated by learning how their actions benefit others:[326] we could ask teachers how they've seen students improve, emphasise what we've noticed, or ask current (or past) students to write thank you cards. Highlighting the impact teachers are having should encourage them to keep going.

> *Help teachers see the value of their efforts*

If teachers start, then stop

We can relaunch the habit

The pressure teachers are under, and the strength of their existing habits, make lasting change a challenge. We can anticipate points at which new habits may slip, like exams and the end of term, reiterating the importance of crucial actions and deferring less urgent ones. Teachers may try an idea once, but conclude it's ineffective: we can encourage them to try again, or to refine the change: "If students found the retrieval quiz results disappointing, how could you prepare them for this next time?" Most importantly, we can keep revisiting the cycle of strategies in this chapter, revising goals, breaking change down, reiterating its value, making it easier and celebrating success – until change sticks.

Refine and relaunch changes when teachers struggle

Applications

- Charlotte wanted teachers to use the school's behaviour management system in a more nuanced way. She could highlight improvements in students' behaviour and learning, and help teachers refine their classroom management strategies until they work, and feel natural.
- Mark wanted experienced colleagues to engage with research, and experiment with new teaching approaches. After discussing a paper, he could ask colleagues what they found interesting; subsequently, he could ask them whether they've applied any of the ideas – and if so, how it helped.
- Jeanette needed Ali (one of her senior leaders) to manage his time and tasks more effectively. She could ask him what difference it's making (and whether he feels more in control) while preparing to relaunch the habit if he struggles.

Key idea

Forming habits is hard; teachers may falter. We can ask ourselves:

- **How do I know what progress teachers are making?**
- **How can I help teachers feel that their efforts are worthwhile?**
- **When should I review and relaunch the change?**

Conclusion

If we want our colleagues to change, behavioural science offers invaluable guidance. Two final suggestions: first, explaining the strategies we are using should help teachers to understand them, and to apply them to get students learning. Second, in this chapter, I've tried to balance my faith that teachers usually know what's best (and should be trusted to do it), with my appreciation of how hard teaching (and change) can be. I hope the chapter helps you support *and trust* your colleagues to improve.

✓ Checklist

Encouraging teachers to change			
Specify the change			
What should we ask teachers to change?	• If there are many things to change ...	**Help teachers focus on a priority**	*Refining objectives before creating assessments.*
	• If we want lasting change ...	**Create a powerful habit**	*Checking what every student has understood each lesson.*
	• If we want immediate change ...	**Create bitesize goals**	*Writing an exit ticket for next week's lesson.*
Inspire and motivate teachers			
How can we convince teachers to change?	• If teachers don't see the value of the change ...	**Show the change addresses challenges they care about**	*Asking teachers about barriers to students' learning.*
	• If teachers don't think the effort is worth it ...	**Highlight benefits and minimise costs**	*"Can we try this for one lesson, then discuss the benefits?"*
	• If teachers don't accept the change ...	**Highlight role models and social norms**	*Asking experienced colleagues to explain how they've used the change.*
Ask teachers to commit to action			
How can we help teachers commit to action?	• If teachers mean to act, then forget ...	**Ask them to commit to a plan**	*"Which lesson could you try this in?"*
		Help them recall their commitments	*"Could you set yourself a reminder?"*
Make starting easy			
How can we encourage teachers to start?	• If teachers aren't sure how to start ...	**Set a default**	*"I suggest asking three of these questions each lesson."*
	• If teachers struggle to start ...	**Practise the change**	*Practising asking questions and responding to student answers.*
Follow-up			
How can we help teachers keep going?	• If teachers don't feel it's worth continuing ...	**Track teachers' progress**	*"Please could you share three great examples of this from your department."*
		Highlight the value of teachers' efforts	*"How have you seen students benefit from this?"*
	• If teachers start, then stop ...	**Review each step, then relaunch the habit**	*"This term we're going to relaunch the change with a couple of tweaks."*

Copyright material from Harry Fletcher-Wood (2022), *Habits of Success: Getting Every Student Learning*, Routledge

Workshop 7: improving teaching

What's the situation?

Jessie is responsible for improving teaching and learning in her school. Her colleagues seem to value professional development sessions, but they rarely act on what they learn. They say they are too busy planning and marking to experiment with their teaching. Jessie recognises how much they have to do, but worries that there will never be a perfect time to focus on making longer-term improvements. (This situation was posed by a busy science teacher in an excellent professional development session.)

What would you suggest?

1) What is the fundamental challenge? What habit or steps would solve it?
2) How would you encourage teachers to act?
3) Do teachers need to commit to action?
4) How can you make it easy?
5) How can you help teachers keep going?

Step 1) Specify the change

Jessie begins with the school's current teaching and learning priority: using questioning to ensure students are thinking hard about the most important ideas. She discusses habits which could promote this with the Teaching and Learning Team. They decide to ask teachers to pause between posing a hard question and inviting a student to answer. Jessie's reading, and her experience, suggest that these pauses encourage students to think harder, and to offer more developed responses. She hopes this will also nudge teachers to re-examine their lesson plans, checking they have planned questions which reveal students' understanding of the crucial ideas.

Jessie then refines the habit to make it powerful. First, she simplifies it, by asking teachers to pick just three key questions each lesson for which a longer pause would be worthwhile. Then she makes the habit fertile (and teachers' actions obvious) by inviting them to discuss the most revealing questions, and most interesting student answers, in department meetings. Finally, Jessie breaks the change into bitesize steps for newer teachers: first, identify a lesson's key points and potential misconceptions; second, write three questions targeting them; third, check the questions with a more experienced colleague.

Step 2) Inspire and motivate teachers to change

Jessie introduces the habit during a professional development session. She begins by highlighting a problem: she asks colleagues to discuss what frustrates them currently about students' verbal answers; they mention incomplete and undeveloped responses. Teachers accept Jessie's explanation of the rationale for longer pauses, and her suggestion that it's a small change with big potential benefits. Finally, Jessie highlights role models who have tried the strategy, inviting two colleagues from the Teaching and Learning Team to describe the benefits they have noticed, barriers they encountered, and how they overcame them.

Step 3) Plan change

Jessie asks teachers to bring plans for upcoming lessons to the professional development session. First, she invites them to identify (or develop) questions which will promote deep thinking, and which merit a longer pause. Then, she asks teachers to set reminders to pause, by marking their plans or PowerPoint. Finally, she suggests inviting a colleague to visit a lesson and see how the strategy is working.

Step 4) Initiate action

Longer pauses can feel unnatural: Jessie uses practice to help her colleagues get used to them. First, she asks teachers to practise in pairs, asking their questions, then pausing for at least three seconds before inviting the "student" to answer. Teachers express concern that students will call out during the pause, so Jessie suggests practising encouraging them to keep thinking using non-verbal signals, like a finger to the lips. When this is working well, Jessie makes practice harder, asking teachers to respond to their partner calling out a correct answer. Practice ensures teachers feel comfortable using the strategy before they try it in the classroom.

Step 5) Follow up

Two groups of teachers are looking for longer pauses in lessons: the colleagues teachers have invited in, and the Teaching and Learning Team, during their routine lesson visits. After two weeks, Jessie asks both groups for anonymous feedback: both examples of good student responses, and any barriers they have observed. She uses these responses to judge whether the habit is sticking, and where colleagues might need further support. They suggest that most teachers are managing longer pauses, and Jessie emails all staff with a few of the best student responses. However, several comments suggest that some questions don't promote the deep thinking she is hoping for. So after half-term, Jessie plans to relaunch the habit, with professional development in departments focused on designing effective questions.

Conclusion

Jessie has made the change manageable for teachers, by picking a discrete but important focus, and giving them time to prepare and practise outside the classroom. The habit seems to be benefiting students: Jessie now plans to build on it, supporting teachers to refine their questioning, and adapt their teaching in response to students' answers.

Conclusion

Every day, in every lesson, teachers are forced to decide "What next?"

The more we help students form habits of success, the easier this becomes.

The more we inspire them to act, the less pressure we have to put on them.

The more detailed their commitments, the more likely they are to act.

The easier it is to start, the more likely they are to do so.

The more we help them keep going, the better the chance that change sticks.

The more we discourage undesirable habits, the more likely they are to stop.

And the more we use these same strategies with teachers, the easier change will be for them.

These principles reflect what I've learned about behavioural science, what I've tried myself, and what I've seen teachers make work. At points, you may have nodded in agreement, shaken your head, and realised that an idea could help you address a nagging problem.

You don't need to agree with everything I've suggested, or accept every example. If you think something wouldn't work in your classroom, and if you think you can improve on what I've suggested, you're almost certainly right. My suggestions are meant to illustrate principles, for you to apply as you see fit.

Nor do you need to try every strategy: one or two carefully chosen changes may be enough to set students on a new path.

Pick a strategy which seems promising. Try it. Track what happens. And keep refining the change until students succeed.

Our students and colleagues can use these strategies too, if we share them. (You can easily share the introduction to this book, or any of the checklists, by going to improvingteaching.co.uk/habits/share).

And we can apply them to our own lives: I suggest ways to do this below.

Teaching is hard. Change is hard. I hope this book makes both a little bit easier.

Please let me know what you try, and what you learn.

Resources

Questions to keep asking

1) What habit, or bitesize goal, would help us to overcome the fundamental challenge we face?
2) How can we show that the change is worthwhile?
3) How can we encourage students to commit to a plan?
4) How can we make it easier to start?
5) How can we help students to keep going?
6) How can we discourage undesirable habits?
7) How can we use these strategies to make change easier for teachers?

Copyright material from Harry Fletcher-Wood (2022), *Habits of Success: Getting Every Student Learning*, Routledge

 Checklist: getting every student learning in a page

What should I ask students to change?	**Specify what students should do:**	
• There are many things to change	**Prioritise the most fundamental challenge**	*Are students focusing? Applying appropriate techniques? Persevering? Contributing?*
• I want students to make a lasting change	**A powerful habit**	*Always plan essays before beginning.*
• I want students to make an immediate change	**A bitesize goal**	*Write for two minutes uninterrupted.*
How can I convince students learning is worthwhile?	**Inspire and motivate students to learn:**	*If I want students to ask more questions . . .*
• Students don't see the value in learning	**Create a need**	*Ask how students feel when they are confused.*
• Students don't think it's worth the effort	**Highlight benefits and minimise costs**	*Encourage students not to miss out on the chance to learn more.*
• Students don't aspire to learn	**Create role models**	*Ask older students to explain how and why they use questions.*
• Students don't accept it	**Highlight social norms**	*Note how many students asked questions last lesson.*
How can I help students commit to action?	**Ask students to commit:**	*If I want a student to de-escalate confrontations, I ask them to . . .*
• Students won't commit to action	**Ask in advance/at landmarks**	*Commit to future action while they're calm.*
• Students mean to act, but don't	**Plan when and how**	*Identify when they will use de-escalation strategies and alternatives.*
	Involve others and prepare prompts	*Share commitments with peers or parents.*
How can I encourage students to start?	**Make starting easy**	*If I want students to start written tasks immediately . . .*
• Students don't know how to start	**Show and tell students how to begin; set defaults**	*Tell students that they must be writing within thirty seconds.*
• Students don't feel confident to start	**Make the first step easier**	*Give students sentence starters or write the first sentence together.*
• Students struggle to start	**Practise**	*Practise writing opening sentences, until students can do so fluently.*
How can I help students keep going?	**Follow-up**	*If I want students to persist when they struggle . . .*
• Students don't see the value of continuing	**Track progress, offer feedback and rewards**	*Track what students are doing; show they are making progress.*
• Students don't feel they belong	**Build identity**	*Celebrate individual and group successes as new social norms.*
• Students start, then stop	**Relaunch the habit**	*Refine every preceding step, and start again.*

Copyright material from Harry Fletcher-Wood (2022), *Habits of Success: Getting Every Student Learning*, Routledge

Using behavioural science ethically

Our job revolves around encouraging, persuading and supporting students to learn: it makes sense to do this as effectively as possible. But is it ethical to use behavioural science to help? Behavioural scientists have suggested five situations in which it is.

1) When goals are shared

If people believe the goal is legitimate, they are usually happy for behavioural science to be used to help achieve it.[327] For example, few object to government efforts to discourage smoking and promote healthy eating. Our goals will usually match those of our students: most want to do their best, they just struggle to act on their intentions. (Even if students don't want to do their best, our goals are likely to match those of the school, parents, and society.) If we are encouraging students to learn more, achieve better, and grow as people, it's ethical to use behavioural science to help.

2) When the change is limited

A researcher asking people to participate in a medical trial needs their informed consent: it's a significant decision. But a researcher tweaking the wording of a medical appointment letter (to encourage attendance) does not: millions of these letters are sent each year already, without undergoing ethical review.[328] Similarly, if we are redesigning our entire behaviour management system, we may want to discuss the changes with parents, students and governors. But we spend our entire day encouraging student effort, learning, and positive behaviour. Small changes to our approach - rephrasing our introduction to a task, encouraging students to set reminders - raise few ethical issues.

3) When it's hard to choose well

It's hard to choose well when the consequences are significant, feedback is delayed, and the link between choices and outcomes is complicated.[329] For example, students' choices about what to do in lessons matter, but the consequence of not focusing now may not be obvious for months or years. (Meanwhile, other influences, such as their peers, may be discouraging good choices.)[330] When choosing well is hard, using behavioural science to help is ethical.[331]

4) When we can't remain neutral

If someone is responsible for organising "the context in which people make decisions," whatever they do or say will influence those decisions.[332] For example, we must sequence lesson activities in some way: some sequences will make learning seem easier, some will make it seem harder. If we cannot be neutral, it's better to apply behavioural science to pursue the best results for students than to pretend neutrality and renounce the positive influence we could have.

Copyright material from Harry Fletcher-Wood (2022), *Habits of Success: Getting Every Student Learning*, Routledge

5) When we're being transparent

Would we be happy to explain our approach to colleagues, parents, and students? Can we create opportunities to do so?[333] Occasionally, "stealthy" interventions are warranted: students may not want to feel they need help; they may respond better to an oblique approach, writing advice for younger students, for example, rather than receiving it themselves.[334] Honesty matters however: approaches which are seen as manipulative are unlikely to work.[335] So it's usually best to be transparent about what we're doing: "I'm asking you to commit to a deadline because it should help you to prioritise the task." Transparency also prepares students to use behavioural science themselves:[336] if they know how habits are formed, for example, they can shape their own. If we are being transparent about our use of behavioural science, we are probably using it ethically.

Conclusion

If we want to review how ethical our approach is, we can ask ourselves (or a colleague or manager):

- Are our goals shared by others?
- How limited is the change?
- How easy is it for students to choose well?
- Can we remain neutral?
- Can we be more transparent?

Our approach can be ethical without answering all of these questions positively: a big change may be justified if we are pursuing shared goals and can't remain neutral, for example. But the more questions we can answer positively, the more assured we can feel about our approach.

Copyright material from Harry Fletcher-Wood (2022), *Habits of Success: Getting Every Student Learning*, Routledge

Using this book with your team

If you want to use this book as a resource for professional development - with a department, group of colleagues or a mentee - you may want to:

1)   Choose a focus:

  o   A student or class
  o   A classroom situation
  o   A lesson, unit or scheme of work (upcoming or recent)
  o   One of the situations described in the book's workshops.

2)   Discuss how the ideas from the book can be applied to the focus, either by:

  o   Working through the book, a chapter at a time; or
  o   Picking one chapter, and working through the questions in the "key ideas" sections; or
  o   Working through a chapter checklist (or the book checklist).

3)   Agree one or two strategies to try, practising them, and committing to use them.

4)   Track their impact, discuss what you've learned, and decide how to build on them - or what to do instead.

Copyright material from Harry Fletcher-Wood (2022), *Habits of Success: Getting Every Student Learning*, Routledge

Using behavioural science to help ourselves

The barriers which stop students from doing things also stop us from doing things. We struggle to act when goals are unclear, when we aren't motivated, when we haven't committed to action and when starting is difficult. We can apply the strategies in this book to our own work, asking ourselves:

- What do I most want to achieve? Am I building a specific habit or pursuing bitesize goals?
- What are the immediate benefits of the change? How can I minimise the immediate costs?
- Have I planned what I will do, when and how? Who could I commit to? What could prompt me to act?
- How can I make the first step easier?
- How will I know if I'm making progress? What will I do if I struggle?

For example, this might lead us to:

- Prioritise a habit - such as checking students' exit tickets as soon as the day is over.
- Identify an immediate benefit (making planning the next lesson easier) and minimising the costs (spending no more than ten minutes on a class's exit tickets).
- Plan when and where to act: picking a specific time (after making tea at the end of the day) and place (the classroom).
- Make starting easy: asking students to pile exit tickets on our desk all facing the same way.
- Track the result: note how many days we managed to do this in a row (and any barriers that that implies - do we struggle most on Friday, for example); sticking with it if it proves useful, adapting our approach if not.

Copyright material from Harry Fletcher-Wood (2022), *Habits of Success: Getting Every Student Learning*, Routledge

Notes

Introduction: How can we get every student learning?

1 Teacher Tapp (2018a). What Teachers Tapped This Week #62–3rd December 2018. Teacher Tapp [blog], http://teachertapp.co.uk/2018/12/what-teachers-tapped-this-week-62-3rd-december-2018/.
2 48% in schools serving the most deprived quintile of students; 30% in schools serving the least deprived quintile; Teacher Tapp (2019). Behaviour: What is going on in schools? (And how does it affect teachers?) – 10th February 2019. Teacher Tapp [blog], https://teachertapp.co.uk/2019/02/behaviour-what-is-really-going-on-in-schools-2019/.
3 28% of primary school teachers reported that learning stopped because of behaviour, as did 31% of secondary school teachers (Teacher Tapp, 2019).
4 Teacher Tapp (2018a).
5 Haydn, T. (2014). To what extent is behaviour a problem in English schools? Exploring the scale and prevalence of deficits in classroom climate. *Review of Education*, 2(1), 47, emphasis original.
6 Heath, C. and Heath, D. (2010). *Switch: How to change things when change is hard*. London: Random House.
7 Ibid., 2.
8 Ibid., 58.
9 Ibid., 58–59.
10 Tze, V.M., Daniels, L.M. and Klassen, R.M. (2016). Evaluating the relationship between boredom and academic outcomes: A meta-analysis. *Educational Psychology Review*, 28(1), 119–144.
11 Caplan, B. (2018). *The Case Against Education: Why the education system is a waste of time and money*. Princeton, NJ: Princeton University Press, 135.
12 Garon-Carrier, G., Boivin, M., Guay, F., Kovas, Y., Dionne, G., Lemelin, J.P., Séguin, J.R., Vitaro, F. and Tremblay, R.E. (2016). Intrinsic motivation and achievement in mathematics in elementary school: A longitudinal investigation of their association. *Child Development*, 87(1), 165–175; van Bergen, E., Snowling, M.J., de Zeeuw, E.L., van Beijsterveldt, C.E., Dolan, C.V. and Boomsma, D.I. (2018). Why do children read more? The influence of reading ability on voluntary reading practices. *Journal of Child Psychology and Psychiatry*, 59(11), 1205–1214.
13 Zimmerman, B. (2002). Becoming a self-regulated learner: An overview. *Theory Into Practice*, 41(2), 64–70.
14 Kruger, J. and Dunning, D. (1999). Unskilled and unaware of it: How difficulties in recognizing one's own incompetence lead to inflated self-assessments. *Journal of Personality and Social Psychology*, 77(6), 1121–1134.
15 Fiorella, L. (2020). The science of habit and its implications for student learning and well-being. *Educational Psychology Review*, 32, 611–612.
16 Wood, W., Quinn, J. and Kashy, D. (2002). Habits in everyday life: Thought, emotion, and action. *Journal of Personality and Social Psychology*, 83(6), 1281–1297.
17 Haidt, J. (2013). *The Righteous Mind: Why good people are divided by politics and religion*. London: Penguin, 131–133.
18 Fiorella (2020), 9.
19 I'm indebted to Dan Cronin for articulating the importance of combining these approaches.
20 Fiorella (2020).

21 Taleb, N. (2018) *Skin in the Game: Hidden asymmetries in daily life*. London: Allen Lane, 150-151.

22 Lavecchia, A.M., Liu, H. and Oreopoulos, P. (2016). Behavioral economics of education: Progress and possibilities. In Eric A. Hanushek, Stephen Machin and Ludger Woessmann (Eds.) *Handbook of the Economics of Education* (Vol. 5). Amsterdam: Elsevier, 1-74.

23 Mook, D. (1983). In defense of external invalidity. *American Psychologist*, 38(4), 386.

24 Gollwitzer, P. and Sheeran, P. (2006). Implementation intentions and goal achievement: A meta-analysis of effects and processes. *Advances in Experimental Social Psychology*, 38, 69-119.

25 Lavecchia, Liu and Oreopoulous (2016).

26 Nosek, B., Cohoon, J., Kidwell, M. and Spies, J. (2015). Estimating the reproducibility of psychological science. *Science*, 349(6251).

27 Nosek et al. (2015), 7.

28 Klein, R., Vianello, M., Hasselman, F., Adams, B., Adams, R., Alper, S., Aveyard, M., Kappes, H., et al. (2018). Many labs 2: Investigating variation in replicability across sample and setting. *Advances in Methods and Practices in Psychological Science*, 1(4), 443-490.

29 For example, goals encourage change and feedback encourages change, but goals and feedback combined are no more powerful than feedback alone. Epton, T., Currie, S. and Armitage, C.J. (2017). Unique effects of setting goals on behavior change: Systematic review and meta-analysis. *Journal of Consulting and Clinical Psychology*, 85(12), 1182-1198.

30 Worth, J. and Van den Brande, J. (2020). Teacher autonomy: How does it relate to job satisfaction and retention? NFER, 12, https://www.nfer.ac.uk/teacher-autonomy-how-does-it-relate-to-job-satisfaction-and-retention/.

31 Gollwitzer and Sheeran (2006).

32 Sunstein, A.R. and Reisch, L.A. (2019). *Trusting Nudges: Towards a bill of rights for nudging*. Abingdon: Routledge, especially Ch. 10.

33 Halpern, D. (2015). *Inside the Nudge Unit: How small changes can make a big difference*. London: WH Allen, 312.

34 Milkman, K., Minson, J. and Volpp, K. (2014). Holding the Hunger Games hostage at the gym: An evaluation of temptation bundling. *Management Science*, 60(2), 283-299.

35 Charness, G. and Gneezy, U. (2009). Incentives to exercise. *Econometrica*, 77(3), 909-931.

36 Lockwood, P. and Kunda, Z. (1997). Superstars and me: Predicting the impact of role models on the self. *Journal of Personality and Social Psychology*, 73(1), 91-103.

1. What should we ask students to change?

37 The approach suggested here is informed by Uncommon Schools' approach to instructional coaching; see Bambrick-Santoyo, P. (2016). *Get Better Faster: A 90-day plan for coaching new teachers*. San Francisco: John Wiley and Sons.

38 Webb, T. and Sheeran, P. (2006). Does changing behavioral intentions engender behavior change? A meta-analysis of the experimental evidence. *Psychological Bulletin*, 132(2), 249-268; Verplanken, B. and Wood, W. (2006). Interventions to break and create consumer habits. *Journal of Public Policy & Marketing*, 25(1), 90-103.

39 Wood, W. and Neal, D. (2007). A new look at habits and the habit-goal interface. *Psychological Review*, 114(4), 843-863.

40 Wood, Quinn and Kashy (2002); Bandura, A. (1982). Self-efficacy mechanism in human agency. *American Psychologist*, 37(2), 122-147.

41 Webb and Sheeran (2006).

42 Deutschman, A. (2005). Change or Die – 1st May 2005. Fast Company [blog], https://www.fastcompany.com/52717/change-or-die.

43 Lally, P., van Jaarsveld, C., Potts, H. and Wardle, J. (2010). How are habits formed: Modelling habit formation in the real world. *European Journal of Social Psychology*, 40(6), 998-1009; Kaushal, N. and Rhodes, R. (2015). Exercise habit formation in new gym members: A longitudinal study. *Journal of Behavioral Medicine*, 38, 652-663.

44 My description of Paul O'Neill's approach is based on Duhigg, C. (2012). *The Power of Habit: Why we do what we do in life and business*. New York: Random House, Ch. 4. I have developed Duhigg's description of a "keystone habit" to emphasise the twin priorities of simplicity and fertility.

45 Ibid., 98.

46 Ibid., 99.

47 Ibid., 106.

48 Ibid., 125.

49 cf. the discussion of "recursive" processes; Yeager, D. and Walton, G. (2011). Social-psychological interventions in education: They're not magic. *Review of Educational Research*, 81(2), 267-301.

50 Bandura (1982); Locke, E.A. and Latham, G.P. (2002). Building a practically useful theory of goal setting and task motivation. *American Psychologist*, 57(9), 705-717.

51 Epton, Currie and Armitage (2017), 1182.

52 Epton, Currie and Armitage (2017); see also Locke and Latham (2002).

53 Larkin, J., McDermott, J., Simon, D. and Simon, H. (1980). Expert and novice performance in solving physics problems. *Science*, 208(4450), 1338. See also Sweller, J. (1988). Cognitive load during problem solving: Effects on learning. *Cognitive Science*, 12(2), 257-285. Perhaps confusingly, the technique Sweller advocates is termed "goal-free problem solving." What this means, however, is avoiding big, distant goals ("Find the length of a specific line," which requires careful step-by-step processing towards that goal) and instead offering an immediate goal ("Find the length of any lines you can").

54 Larkin et al. (1980), 1339.

55 Larkin et al. (1980).

56 For the principle, see Service, O., Hallsworth, M., Halpern, D., Algate, F., Gallagher, R., Nguyen, S., Ruda, S. and Sanders, M. (2014). EAST: Four simple ways to apply behavioural insights. Behavioural Insights Team, https://www.bi.team/publications/east-four-simple-ways-to-apply-behavioural-insights/. For a specific example in students' responses to feedback, see Nelson, M. and Schunn, C. (2008). The nature of feedback: How different types of peer feedback affect writing performance. *Instructional Science*, 37(4), 375-401.

57 I'm indebted to Susie Fraser and Josh Goodrich for their observations on this point.

58 Barton, C. (2018). *How I Wish I'd Taught Maths: Lessons learned from research, conversations with experts, and 12 years of mistakes*. Woodbridge: John Catt, 263-265.

59 Epton, Currie and Armitage (2017).

2. How can we convince students to learn?

60 Leventhal, H., Singer, R. and Jones, S. (1965). Effects of fear and specificity of recommendation upon attitudes and behavior. *Journal of Personality and Social Psychology*, 2(1), 20-29. Whether they acted also depended on specific guidance about where and when to get vaccinations, which we discuss in Chapter 3.

61 Heath, C. and Heath, D. (2017). *The Power of Moments: Why certain experiences have extraordinary impact*. New York: Simon and Schuster, 97-102.

62 Bransford, J., Sherwood, R., Hasselbring, T., Klinzer, C. and Williams, S. (1990). Anchored instruction: Why we need it and how technology can help (Chapter 5). In Nix, D. and Spiro, R. (Eds.) *Cognition, Education, and Multimedia: Exploring ideas in high technology*. Hillsdale, NJ: Lawrence Erlbaum Associates, 117.

63 Meyer, D. (2015). "If Math Is The Aspirin, Then How Do You Create The Headache?" – 17th June 2015 [blog], https://blog.mrmeyer.com/2015/if-math-is-the-aspirin-then-how-do-you-create-the-headache/.

64 Meyer (2015).

65 Meyer, D. (n.d.) Directory of Mathematical Headaches. https://docs.google.com/document/d/1JZmjliq JikVD69y5ZY8wOV8Ml47lBdH1DrhLiBeKQh8/edit.

66 Mayer, R. (2004). Should there be a three-strikes rule against pure discovery learning? The case for guided methods of instruction. *American Psychologist*, 59(1), 14-19.

67 Ryan, R. and Deci, E. (2000). Self-determination theory and the facilitation of intrinsic motivation, social development, and well-being. *American Psychologist*, 55(1), 71.

68 Larkin et al. (1980); Sweller (1988).

69 For the crucial role knowledge plays in understanding, see, for example, Recht, D.R. and Leslie, L. (1988). Effect of prior knowledge on good and poor readers' memory of text. *Journal of Educational Psychology*, 80, 16-20, or a summary in Willingham, D. (2009). *Why Don't Students Like School? A cognitive scientist answers questions about how the mind works and what it means for the classroom*. San Francisco, CA: Jossey-Bass, Ch. 2.

70 Kirschner, P. and van Merriënboer, J. (2013). Do learners really know best? Urban legends in education. *Educational Psychologist*, 48(3), 169-183.

71 Dunlosky, J., Rawson, K., Marsh, E., Mitchell, J. and Willingham, D. (2013). Improving students' learning with effective learning techniques: Promising directions from cognitive and educational psychology. *Psychological Science in the Public Interest*, 14(1), 4–58.

72 Epton, Currie and Armitage (2017).

73 Locke and Latham (2002).

74 Briscese, G. and Tan, C. (2018). Applying Behavioural Insights to Labour Markets. Behavioural Insights Team, https://www.bi.team/publications/applying-behavioural-insights-to-labour-markets/.

75 Hershfield, H.E., Goldstein, D.G., Sharpe, W.F., Fox, J., Yeykelis, L., Carstensen, L.L. and Bailenson, J.N., (2011). Increasing saving behavior through age-progressed renderings of the future self. *Journal of Marketing Research*, 48(SPL), S23–S37.

76 Behavioural Insights Team (2019). Annual Report 2017–18. Behavioural Insights Team, https://www.bi.team/publications/the-behavioural-insights-team-annual-report-2017-18/.

77 Yeager and Walton (2011), 284, 290.

78 Canning, E. and Harackiewicz, J. (2015). Teach it, don't preach it: The differential effects of directly communicated and self-generated utility–value information. *Motivation Science*, 1(1), 47–71.

79 Yeager, D.S., Henderson, M.D., Paunesku, D., Walton, G.M., D'Mello, S., Spitzer, B.J. and Duckworth, A.L. (2014). Boring but important: A self-transcendent purpose for learning fosters academic self-regulation. *Journal of Personality and Social Psychology*, 107(4), 568–569.

80 Kahneman, D. (2011). *Thinking, Fast and Slow*. London: Penguin, 367.

81 Read, D., Loewenstein, G. and Kalyanarman, S. (1999). Mixing virtue and vice: Combining the immediacy effect and the diversification heuristic. *Journal of Behavioral Decision Making*, 12, 257–273.

82 Hume, S., O'Reilly, F., Groot, B., Chande, R., Sanders, M., Hollingsworth, A., Ter Meer, J., Barnes, J., Booth, S., Kozman, E. and Soon, X. (2018). Improving engagement and attainment in maths and English courses: Insights from behavioural research: Research and project report. Department for Education, 77, https://www.gov.uk/government/publications/improving-engagement-and-attainment-in-maths-and-english-courses.

83 Levitt, S.D., List, J.A., Neckermann, S. and Sadoff, S. (2016). The behavioralist goes to school: Leveraging behavioral economics to improve educational performance. *American Economic Journal: Economic Policy*, 8(4), 183–219.

84 For the motivating effects of autonomy, mastery and relatedness see Ryan and Deci (2000).

85 Kahneman, D., Knetsch, J.L. and Thaler, R.H. (1991). Anomalies: The endowment effect, loss aversion, and status quo bias. *Journal of Economic Perspectives*, 5(1), 193–206. One experiment in this paper shows that people want twice as much money to give up (lose) a mug than they would be willing to pay to buy it, an illustration that loss is much less attractive than gain is attractive. See also, Kahneman (2011), 368; Kuhberger, A. (1998). The influence of framing on risky decisions: A meta-analysis. *Organizational Behavior and Human Decision Processes*, 75(1), 23–55.

86 Levitt et al. (2016). The effect was directional but not significant (possibly because the students were not actually given the money to hold on to). It is included here as a school-based example of a widely accepted principle; see Kahneman (2011), Ch. 26.

87 Cialdini, R. (2007). *Influence: The psychology of persuasion*. New York: HarperBusiness.

88 Worchel, S. (1992). Beyond a commodity theory: Analysis of censorship: When abundance and personalism enhance scarcity effects. *Basic and Applied Social Psychology*, 13(1), 79–92.

89 Rothman, A., Bartels, R., Wlaschin, J. and Salovey, P. (2006). The strategic use of gain- and loss-framed messages to promote healthy behavior: How theory can inform practice. *Journal of Communications* (56), S202–S220.

90 Ibid.

91 Bandura (1982); Gibson, D. (2004). Role models in career development: New directions for theory and research. *Journal of Vocational Behaviour*, 65(1), 134–156; Lockwood and Kunda (1997).

92 Behavioural Insights Team (2015). Behavioural Insights and the Somerset Challenge, https://www.bi.team/publications/behavioural-insights-and-the-somerset-challenge/; de Wit, J., Das, E. and Vet, R. (2008). What works best: Objective statistics or a personal testimonial? An assessment of the persuasive effects of different types of message evidence on risk perception. *Health Psychology*, 27(1), 110–115.

93 Baars, S., Mulcahy, E. and Bernardes, E. (2016). The underrepresentation of white working class boys in higher education: The role of widening participation. London: LKMCo; Durantini, M., Albarracín, D., Mitchell, A., Earl, A. and Gillette, J. (2006). Conceptualizing the influence of social agents of behavior change: A meta-analysis of the effectiveness of HIV-prevention interventionists for different groups. *Psychological Bulletin*, 132(2), 212–248.

94 An effect which is separate from the effect of having a supportive family. Bryant, A.L. and Zimmerman, M.A. (2003). Role models and psychosocial outcomes among African American adolescents. *Journal of Adolescent Research*, 18(1), 36–67.

95 See, for example, Anderson, K. and Cavallaro, D. (2002) Parents or pop culture? Children's heroes and role models. *Childhood Education*, 78(3), 161–168; Bryant and Zimmerman (2003), 46; Clark, C., Osborne, S. and Dugdale, G. (2009). Reaching out with role models role models and young people's reading. National Literacy Trust, https://literacytrust.org.uk/research-services/research-reports/reaching-out-role-models-role-models-and-young-peoples-reading-2009/; Kniveton, B. (2004). The influences and motivations on which students base their choice of career. *Research in Education*, 72, 47–57.

96 Gibson (2004).

97 Clark, Osborne and Dugdale (2009).

98 Ibid.

99 For the importance of similarity and relevance see Bandura (1982), Gibson (2004); for gender and ethnicity, Anderson and Cavallaro (2002); for future plans, Lockwood and Kunda (1997).

100 Fisher, D., Frey, N. and Lapp, D. (2011a). Coaching middle-level teachers to think aloud improves comprehension instruction and student reading achievement. *The Teacher Educator*, 46(3), 231–243.

101 Bandura (1982); Siegle, D. and McCoach, B. (2007). Increasing student mathematics self-efficacy through teacher training. *Journal of Advanced Academics*, 18(2), 278–312, this study also set clear goals and highlighted students' successes.

102 Lockwood and Kunda (1997).

103 Bursztyn, L. and Jensen, R. (2015). How does peer pressure affect educational investments? *The Quarterly Journal of Economics*, 130(3), 1329–1367.

104 Behavioural Insights Team (2015).

105 Behavioural Insights Team (2017).

106 Lockwood and Kunda (1997); Rogers, T. and Feller, A. (2016). Discouraged by peer excellence: Exposure to exemplary peer performance causes quitting. *Psychological Science*, 27(3), 365–374.

107 Burgess, S. (2016). Michelle Obama and an English school: The power of inspiration. https://simonburgesseconomics.co.uk/wp-content/uploads/2016/06/EGA-paper-20160627.pdf.

108 Lin-Siegler, X., Ahn, J.N., Chen, J., Fang, F.F.A. and Luna-Lucero, M. (2016). Even Einstein struggled: Effects of learning about great scientists' struggles on high school students' motivation to learn science. *Journal of Educational Psychology*, 108(3), 314–328.

109 Anderson and Cavallaro (2002), Clark, Osborne and Dugdale (2009); Kniveton (2004).

110 Aronson, E. (1999). The power of self-persuasion. *American Psychologist*, 54(11), 875–884.

111 Yeager and Walton (2011).

112 Aronson (1999).

113 Researchers call expected behaviour the "injunctive norm" and prevalent behaviour the "descriptive norm." House, B. (2017). How do social norms influence prosocial development? *Current Opinion in Psychology*, 20, 87–91.

114 Cialdini, R., Reno, R. and Kallgren, C. (1990). A focus theory of normative conduct: Recycling the concept of norms to reduce littering in public places. *Journal of Personality and Social Psychology*, 58(6), 1015–1026.

115 Keizer, K., Lindenburg, S. and Steg, L. (2008). The spreading of disorder. *Science*, 322(5908), 1681–1685.

116 Heath and Heath (2010), 17.

117 For discussion of differing expectations (not in a school context), see Cialdini, Reno and Kallgren (1990), 1025.

118 Heath and Heath (2010), 17.

119 Nuthall, G. (2007). *The Hidden Lives of Learners*. Wellington: New Zealand Council for Educational Research, 37.

120 Ferraro, P.J., Miranda, J.J. and Price, M.K. (2011). The persistence of treatment effects with norm-based policy instruments: Evidence from a randomized environmental policy experiment. *American Economic Review*, 101(3), 318–322.

121 Nuthall (2007), 37.

122 Didau, D. (2018). Teaching matters, but there are more important things to get right – 8th July 2018. Learning Spy [blog], https://learningspy.co.uk/featured/teaching-maters-but-there-are-more-important-things-to-get-right/.

123 Sacerdote, B. (2001). Peer effects with random assignment: Results for Dartmouth roommates. *The Quarterly Journal of Economics*, 116(2), 681-704.

124 Bursztyn and Jensen (2015).

125 Commonwealth of Australia (2018). Nudge vs Superbugs: A behavioural economics trial to reduce the overprescribing of antibiotics, https://www1.health.gov.au/internet/main/publishing.nsf/Content/Nudge-vs-Superbugs-behavioural-economics-trial-to-reduce-overprescribing-antibiotics-June-2018.

126 Bursztyn and Jensen (2015).

127 Bertrand, M., Mullainathan, S. and Shafir, E. (2006). Behavioral economics and marketing in aid of decision making among the poor. *Journal of Public Policy & Marketing*, 25(1), 10.

128 Abrahamse, W. and Shwom, R. (2018). Domestic energy consumption and climate change mitigation. *WIREs Climate Change*, 9(14), e525.

129 Kahan, D. (2000). Gentle nudges vs. hard shoves: Solving the sticky norms problem. *The University of Chicago Law Review*, 67(3), 607-645.

130 Kahan (2000).

131 Ibid.

132 Sparkman, G. and Walton, G.M. (2017). Dynamic norms promote sustainable behavior, even if it is counternormative. *Psychological Science*, 28(11), 1663-1674.

133 Paluck, E.L. (2009). Reducing intergroup prejudice and conflict using the media: A field experiment in Rwanda. *Journal of Personality and Social Psychology*, 96(3), 574-587.

3. How can we help students to commit to action?

134 Wood, W. and Neal, D. (2016). Healthy through habit: Interventions for initiating & maintaining health behavior change. *Behavioral Science & Policy*, 2(1), 71-83.

135 Lovell, O. (2018a). When the space, retrieve, interleave formula doesn't work! - 2nd April 2018 [blog], http://www.ollielovell.com/olliesclassroom/fail-v1/.

136 Thaler, R. and Benartzi, S. (2004). Save more tomorrow: Using behavioral economics to increase employee saving. *Journal of Political Economy*, 112(1), 164-187.

137 Giné, X., Karlan, D. and Zinman, J. (2010). Put your money where your butt is: A commitment contract for smoking cessation. *American Economic Journal: Applied Economics*, 2(4), 213-235.

138 Gilovich, T., Kerr, M. and Medvec, V. (1993). Effect of temporal perspective on subjective confidence. *Journal of Personality and Social Psychology*, 64(4), 552-560.

139 Ariely, D. and Wertenbroch, K. (2002). Procrastination, deadlines, and performance: Self-control by precommitment. *Psychological Science*, 13(3), 219-224.

140 Thompson, S., Michaelson, J., Abdallah, S., Johnson, V., Morris, D., Riley, K. and Simms, A. (2011). *"Moments of change" as opportunities for influencing behaviour: A report to the Department for Environment, Food and Rural Affairs*. London: Defra.

141 Data on diets only relates to dates, not to individuals' birthdays; Dai, H., Milkman, K. and Riis, J. (2014). The fresh start effect: Temporal landmarks motivate aspirational behavior. *Management Science*, 60(10), 2563-2582.

142 Heath and Heath (2017), Ch. 8.

143 Yeager and Walton (2011).

144 Gollwitzer and Sheeran (2006), 69, 75-81.

145 Milkman, K.L., Beshears, J., Choi, J.J., Laibson, D. and Madrian, B.C. (2011). Using implementation intentions prompts to enhance influenza vaccination rates. *Proceedings of the National Academy of Sciences*, 108(26), 10415-10420.

146 Gollwitzer and Sheeran (2006); Heath and Heath (2017), 185; Rogers, T., Milkman, K., John, L. and Norton, M. (2015). Beyond good intentions: Prompting people to make plans improves follow-through on important tasks. *Behavioral Science & Policy*, 1(2), 33-41.

147 Duckworth, A.L., Kirby, T.A., Gollwitzer, A. and Oettingen, G. (2013). From fantasy to action: Mental contrasting with implementation intentions (MCII) improves academic performance in children. *Social Psychological and Personality Science*, 4(6), 745-753.

148 Rogers et al. (2015).

149 Lally, P. and Gardner, B. (2013). Promoting habit formation. *Health Psychology Review*, 7(sup1), S137–S158.

150 Wood and Neal (2016).

151 Pink, D. (2018). *When: The scientific secrets of perfect timing*. Edinburgh: Canongate, Ch. 1.

152 Burger, N., Charness, G. and Lynham, J. (2011). Field and online experiments on self-control. *Journal of Economic Behavior & Organization*, 77, 393–404.

153 Pink (2018), Ch. 1.

154 Gollwitzer and Sheeran (2006); Lally and Gardner (2013); Rogers et al. (2015)

155 Gollwitzer and Sheeran (2006).

156 Rogers et al. (2015).

157 Burger, N. and Lynham, J. (2010). Betting on weight loss . . . and losing: Personal gambles as commitment mechanisms. *Applied Economics Letters*, 17(12), 1161–1166.

158 Nyer, P. and Dellande, S. (2010). Public commitment as a motivator for weight loss. *Psychology & Marketing*, 27(1), 1–12.

159 Rogers et al. (2015), 35.

160 Bursztyn and Jensen (2015): whether students accepted help was not actually made public, but some were told that it would be, while others were told it would not; the statement made here describes the effect among students who were taking both honours and non-honours courses and reflects whether they were asked in the former or the latter.

161 Ibid.; see also Nyer and Dellande (2010).

162 Austin, J., Sigurdsson, S. and Rubin, Y. (2006). An examination of the effects of delayed versus immediate prompts on safety belt use. *Environment and Behavior*, 38(1), 140–149.

163 Although it was suggested that the resulting submissions were better: Hand, E. (2016). No pressure: NSF test finds eliminating deadlines halves number of grant proposals. *Science*. 15th April, https://www.sciencemag.org/news/2016/04/no-pressure-nsf-test-finds-eliminating-deadlines-halves-number-grant-proposals#.

164 Tu, Y. and Soman, D. (2014). The categorization of time and its impact on task initiation. *Journal of Consumer Research*, 41(3), 810–822.

165 Pink (2018), Ch. 3.

166 Tu and Soman (2014).

167 Ryan and Deci (2000).

168 Ariely and Wertenbroch (2002).

169 Burger, Charness and Lynham (2011).

170 Castleman, B. and Page, L. (2015). Summer nudging: Can personalized text messages and peer mentor outreach increase college going among low-income high school graduates? *Journal of Economic Behavior & Organization*, 115, 144–160.

171 Gawande, A. (2010). *The Checklist Manifesto: How to get things right*. London: Profile.

172 Behavioural Insights Team (2019).

173 Fletcher-Wood, H. (2016). *Ticked Off: Checklists for students, teachers and school leaders*. Bancyfelin: Crown House.

174 Rogers, T. and Feller, A. (2018). Reducing student absences at scale by targeting parents' misbeliefs. *Nature Human Behaviour*, 2(5), 335–342.

175 Groot, B., Sanders, M., Rogers, T. and Bloomenthal, E. (2017). I get by with a little help from my friends: Two field experiments on social support and attendance in further education colleges in the UK. Behavioural Insights Team, https://www.behaviouralinsights.co.uk/wp-content/uploads/2017/06/Study-Supporter-Working-Paper_2017.pdf; Hume et al. (2018); Miller, S., Davison, J., Yohanis, J., Sloan, S., Gildea, A. and Thurston, A. (2016). Texting parents: Evaluation report and executive summary. Education Endowment Fund, https://educationendowmentfoundation.org.uk/projects-and-evaluation/projects/texting-parents/. A more recent attempt to apply Groot et al.'s approach in further education colleges failed to replicate these findings, however, this study faced many practical barriers (like students choosing not to sign up), which a classroom teacher or school could avoid by using the existing school system for text messages. Scandone, B., Wishart, R., Griggs, J., Smith, N., Burridge, H., Lepanjuuri, K., Hall, P., Chadwick, T. and Averill, P. (2020). Texting students and study supporters (Project SUCCESS). Education Endowment Foundation, https://educationendowmentfoundation.org.uk/projects-and-evaluation/projects/texting-students-and-study-supporters/.

176 Lovell, O. (2018b). Implementation intentions and action triggers: Moving beyond "Well, make sure you do it next time" – 15th November 2018 [blog], http://www.ollielovell.com/olliesclassroom/imple mentation-intentions-action-triggers/.

177 Rogers et al. (2015); Damgaard, M. and Nielsen, H. (2018). Nudging in education. *Economics of Education Review*, 64, 313–342.

4. How can we encourage students to start?

178 Hume et al. (2018).

179 Aamodt, M. and McShane, T. (1992). A meta-analytic investigation of the effect of various test item characteristics on test scores and test completion times. *Public Personnel Management*, 21(2), 151–160.

180 Nunes, J. and Dreze, X. (2006). The endowed progress effect: How artificial advancement increases effort. *Journal of Consumer Research*, 32(4), 504–512.

181 Lemov, D. (2015a). *Teach Like a Champion 2.0*. San Francisco: Jossey-Bass, 417.

182 Ibid., 414.

183 Sweller, J., van Merriënboer J.J. and Paas F.G. (1998). Cognitive architecture and instructional design. *Educational Psychology Review*, 10, 251–296.

184 Barton (2018), Ch. 6.

185 Renkl, A., Hilbert, T. and Schworm, S. (2009). Example-based learning in heuristic domains: A cognitive load theory account. *Educational Psychology Review*, 21(1), 68.

186 Isaac, A. (2018). Auto-enrolment pensions are a hit – with one major catch. *The Daily Telegraph*, 8th May, https://www.telegraph.co.uk/business/2018/05/08/auto-enrolment-pensions-hit-one-major-catch/.

187 Pichert, D. and Katsikopoulos, K. (2008). Green defaults: Information presentation and proenvironmental behaviour. *Journal of Environmental Psychology*, 28, 63–73.

188 Bertrand, Mullainathan and Shafir (2006).

189 Sweller, J., Ayres, P.L., Kalyuga, S. and Chandler, P.A. (2003). The expertise reversal effect. *Educational Psychologist*, 38(1), 23–31.

190 Keller, P., Harlam, B., Loewenstein, G. and Volpp, K. (2011). Enhanced active choice: A new method to motivate behavior change. *Journal of Consumer Psychology*, 21, 376–383.

191 Sweller, van Merriënboer and Paas (1998).

192 Willingham (2009), Ch. 2.

193 Kennedy, M. (2015). Parsing the practice of teaching. *Journal of Teacher Education*, 67(1), 14.

194 Soderstrom, N. and Bjork, R. (2015). Learning versus performance: An integrative review. *Perspectives on Psychological Science*, 10(2), 176–199; van Merriënboer, J., Kester, L. and Paas, F. (2006). Teaching complex rather than simple tasks: Balancing intrinsic and germane load to enhance transfer of learning. *Applied Cognitive Psychology*, 20(3), 343–352.

195 Ericsson, A. and Pool, R. (2016). *Peak: Secrets from the new science of expertise*. London: Bodley Head. The authors' claim that practice is the sole ingredient to expertise is an overstatement. Nonetheless, even the strongest critics agree that it plays an important role. See, for example, Macnamara, B.N., Hambrick, D.Z., Frank, D.J., King, M.J., Burgoyne, A.P. and Meinz, E.J. (2018). The deliberate practice view: An evaluation of definitions, claims, and empirical evidence (Ch. 9). In Hambrick, D.Z., Campitelli, G. and Macnamara, B.N. (Eds.) *The Science of Expertise: Behavioral, neural, and genetic approaches to complex skill*, Abingdon: Routledge.

196 McGaghie, W.C., Issenberg, S.B., Cohen, M.E.R., Barsuk, J.H. and Wayne, D.B. (2011). Does simulation-based medical education with deliberate practice yield better results than traditional clinical education? A meta-analytic comparative review of the evidence. *Academic Medicine: Journal of the Association of American Medical Colleges*, 86(6), 706–711.

197 Duhigg (2012), Ch. 5.

198 Heath and Heath (2017), Ch. 9.

199 Ericsson and Pool (2016).

200 Binder, C. (1996). Behavioral fluency: Evolution of a new paradigm. *The Behavior Analyst*, 19(2), 163–197.

201 Lemov, D., Woolway, E. and Yezzi, K. (2012). *Practice Perfect: 42 rules for getting better at getting better*. San Francisco: Jossey-Bass, 25–29.

202 Lemov (2015a), 373–375.

5. How can we help students to keep going?

203 Wood and Neal (2016).

204 Gardner, B. (2014). A review and analysis of the use of "habit" in understanding, predicting and influencing health-related behaviour. *Health Psychology Review*, 9(3), 277-295; Wood and Neal (2007).

205 Gardner (2014); Kaushal and Rhodes (2015).

206 Lemov, D. (2015b). Hunting versus fishing – 24th July. Teach Like a Champion [blog], https://teachlikeachampion.com/blog/hunting-versus-fishing/.

207 Ariely, D. (2013). *The Honest Truth About Dishonesty: How we lie to everyone – especially ourselves.* London: Harper Perennial.

208 Panadero, E., Jonsson, A. and Botella, J. (2017). Effects of self-assessment on self-regulated learning and self-efficacy: Four meta-analyses. *Educational Research Review*, 22, 74-98.

209 Sadler, D. (1989). Formative assessment and the design of instructional systems. *Instructional Science*, 18(2), 119-144.

210 Ryan and Deci (2000); Lepper, M., Henderlong Corpus, J. and Iyengar, S. (2005). Intrinsic and extrinsic motivational orientations in the classroom: Age differences and academic correlates. *Journal of Educational Psychology*, 97(2), 184-196.

211 Charness and Gneezy (2009).

212 Jalava, N., Joensen, J.S. and Pellas, E. (2015). Grades and rank: Impacts of non-financial incentives on test performance. *Journal of Economic Behavior & Organization*, 115, 161-196; Levitt et al. (2016); Springer, M.G., Rosenquist, B.A. and Swain, W.A. (2015). Monetary and nonmonetary student incentives for tutoring services: A randomized controlled trial. *Journal of Research on Educational Effectiveness*, 8(4), 453-474.

213 Service et al. (2014).

214 Lavecchia, Liu and Oreopoulous (2016), 36.

215 Fryer, R.G. (2011). Financial incentives and student achievement: Evidence from randomized trials. *The Quarterly Journal of Economics*, 126(4), 1755-1798.

216 Ibid., 1791-1792: note that the two groups of students were of different ages.

217 Wood and Neal (2016), 75.

218 Lemov (2015a), 435.

219 Wood and Neal (2016), 75.

220 Lally and Gardner (2013).

221 Wood and Neal (2016), 75.

222 Levitt et al. (2016).

223 A review suggests girls and high-attaining students benefit more; Gneezy, U., Meier, S. and Rey-Biel, P. (2011). When and why incentives (don't) work to modify behavior. *The Journal of Economic Perspectives*, 25(4), 191-209. But more recent experiments have found greater benefits for boys (Levitt et al., 2016) and lower-attaining students (Sibieta, L., Greaves, E. and Sianesi, B. (2014). Increasing pupil motivation: Evaluation report and executive summary. Education Endowment Foundation, https://educationendowmentfoundation.org.uk/projects-and-evaluation/projects/increasing-pupil-motivation/).

224 Jalava, Joensen and Pellas (2015).

225 Fryer, R.G. (2017). The production of human capital in developed countries: Evidence from 196 randomized field experiments. In E. Duflo and A. Banerjee (Eds.) *Handbook of Economic Field Experiments* (Vol. 2). North-Holland, 95-322.

226 Gneezy, Meier and Rey-Biel (2011).

227 Bursztyn and Jensen (2015).

228 Springer, Rosenquist and Swain (2015).

229 Gneezy, Meier and Rey-Biel (2011); Lally and Gardner (2013); Wood and Neal (2016).

230 Amabile, T. and Kramer, S. (2011). The power of small wins. *Harvard Business Review*. May.

231 Hulleman, C. and Harackiewicz, J. (2009). Promoting interest and performance in high school science classes. *Science*. 326(5958), Supplement, 18.

232 Ibid., Supplement, 11.

233 Bandura (1982); Wood and Neal (2007), 852.

234 Bandura (1982); Lally and Gardner (2013).

235 Lally and Gardner (2013).

236 Panadero, Jonsson and Botella (2017).

237 Siegle and McCoach (2007).

238 McCrea, E. (2019). *Making Every Maths Lesson Count: Six principles to support great maths teaching.* Bancyfelin: Crown House.

239 Gilovich, Kerr and Medvec (1993).

240 Heath and Heath (2017), Ch. 8.

241 Baumeister, R.F. and Leary, M.R. (1995). The need to belong: Desire for interpersonal attachments as a fundamental human motivation. *Psychological Bulletin,* 117(3), 497-529.

242 Haidt (2013), 221.

243 Haidt (2013), 258, 275; Ryan and Deci (2000), 73.

244 Walton, G.M., Cohen, G.L., Cwir, D. and Spencer, S.J. (2012). Mere belonging: The power of social connections. *Journal of Personality and Social Psychology,* 102(3), 513-532.

245 Sanders, M., Chonaire, A.N., Carr, D., Heal, J. and Anik, L. (2017). Increasing social trust with an ice-breaking exercise: An RCT carried out with NCS participants. Behavioural Insights Team. http://www.behaviouralinsights.co.uk/wp-content/uploads/2017/03/Increasing-social-trust.pdf.

246 Todd, A. and Galinsky, A. (2014). Perspective-taking as a strategy for improving intergroup relations: Evidence, mechanisms, and qualifications. *Social and Personality Psychology Compass,* 8(7), 374-387.

247 Gehlbach, H., Brinkworth, M.E., King, A.M., Hsu, L.M., McIntyre, J. and Rogers, T. (2016). Creating birds of similar feathers: Leveraging similarity to improve teacher-student relationships and academic achievement. *Journal of Educational Psychology,* 108(3), 342-352.

248 Cook, C., Fiat, A., Larson, M., Daikos, C., Slemrod, T., Holland, E., Thayer, A. and Renshaw, T. (2018). Positive greetings at the door: Evaluation of a low-cost, high-yield proactive classroom management strategy. *Journal of Positive Behavior Interventions,* 20(3), 149-159.

249 Yeager, D., Purdie-Vaughns, V., Garcia, J., Apfel, N., Brzustoski, P., Master, A., Hessert, W., Williams, M. and Cohen, G. (2014). Breaking the cycle of mistrust: Wise interventions to provide critical feedback across the racial divide. *Journal of Experimental Psychology: General,* 143(2), 809.

250 Ibid.

251 Haidt (2013), 277.

252 Walton et al. (2012).

253 Haidt (2013).

254 Haidt, J., Seder, J.P. and Kesebir, S. (2008). Hive psychology, happiness, and public policy. *The Journal of Legal Studies,* 37(S2), S133-S156.

255 Maruna, S. (2011). Reentry as a rite of passage. *Punishment & Society,* 13(1), 3-28.

256 Silkwood School (n.d.). Moments that Matter [web page], https://www.silkwood.qld.edu.au/silkwood-way/festivals-transition-ceremonies-and-camps.

257 Fisher, D., Frey, N. and Lapp, D. (2011b). Focusing on the participation and engagement gap: A case study on closing the achievement gap. *Journal of Education for Students Placed at Risk,* 16(1), 59.

258 Epton, T., Harris, P.R., Kane, R., van Koningsbruggen, G.M. and Sheeran, P. (2015). The impact of self-affirmation on health-behavior change: A meta-analysis. *Health Psychology,* 34(3), 187-196.

259 Cohen, G.L., Garcia, J., Purdie-Vaughns, V., Apfel, N. and Brzustoski, P. (2009). Recursive processes in self-affirmation: Intervening to close the minority achievement gap. *Science,* 324(5925), 400-403.

260 Haidt, Seder and Kesebir (2008), S147-S148.

261 Maruna (2011).

262 Lally et al. (2010). A study of gym attendance reached similar conclusions; Kaushal and Rhodes (2015).

263 Webb and Sheeran (2006).

264 Wood and Neal (2016), 71-72.

265 Acland, D. and Levy, M.R. (2015). Naiveté, projection bias, and habit formation in gym attendance. *Management Science,* 61(1), 146-160.

266 cf. Lemov (2015a), 301.

267 Milkman, Minson and Volpp (2014), 12.

268 I'm indebted to Josh Goodrich for this observation.

6. How can we help students to stop?

269 Ariely (2013), 14ff.

270 Atkins, M.S., McKay, M.M., Frazier, S.L., Jakobsons, L.J., Arvanitis, P., Cunningham, T., Brown, C. and Lambrecht, L. (2002). Suspensions and detentions in an urban, low-income school: Punishment or reward? *Journal of Abnormal Child Psychology,* 30(4), 361-371.

271 Lemov (2015a), 406.
272 McInerney, L. (2012). Ms McInerney's "Book of Consequences" Detention System – 17th November 2012. LauraMcinerney.com [blog], https://lauramcinerney.com/ms-mcinerneys-book-of-consequences-detention-system/.
273 Lally and Gardner (2013); Webb, T., Sheeran, P. and Luszczynska, A. (2009). Planning to break unwanted habits: Habit strength moderates implementation intention effects on behaviour change. *British Journal of Social Psychology*, 48, 507–523.
274 Gibson (2004).
275 Valente, T. (1996). Social network thresholds in the diffusion of innovations. *Social Networks*, 18(1), 69–89.
276 Keizer, Lindenburg and Steg (2008).
277 Ariely (2013), 198–204.
278 Atkins et al. (2002).
279 Ibid., 368.
280 Webb, Sheeran and Luszczynska (2009).
281 Fiorella (2020).
282 Gardner (2014); Kaushal and Rhodes (2015).
283 Fiorella (2020), 4–5.
284 Harford, T. (2019). Lunch with the FT. Richard Thaler: "If you want people to do something, make it easy." *Financial Times*, 2nd August.
285 Hawton, K., Simkin, S., Dodd, S., Pocock, P., Bernal, W., Gunnell, D. and Kapur, N. (2013). Long term effect of reduced pack sizes of paracetamol on poisoning deaths and liver transplant activity in England and Wales: Interrupted time series analyses. *British Medical Journal*, 346, f403.
286 McInerney (2012).

7. How can we encourage teachers to change?

287 Sims, S., Hobbiss, M. and Allen, R. (2020). Habit formation limits growth in teacher effectiveness: A review of converging evidence from neuroscience and social science. *Review of Education*, 9(1), 3–23.
288 Berliner, D. (1988). *The Development of Expertise in Pedagogy*. Charles W. Hunt Memorial Lecture presented at the Annual Meeting of the American Association of Colleges for Teacher Education (New Orleans, LA, February 17–20).
289 Nuthall, G. (2005). The cultural myths and realities of classroom teaching and learning: A personal journey. *Teachers College Record*, 107(5), 927.
290 Elmore, R. (1996). Getting to scale with good educational practice. *Harvard Educational Review*, 66(1), 4.
291 Kennedy, M. (2010). Attribution error and the quest for teacher quality. *Educational Researcher*, 39(8), 591–598.
292 Andrews, M. (2018). Implementing Public Policy: Is it possible to escape the "Public Policy Futility" trap? – 6th December 2018. Building State Capability [blog], https://buildingstatecapability.com/2018/12/06/implementing-public-policy-is-it-possible-to-escape-the-public-policy-futility-trap/.
293 Wiliam, D. (2016). *Leadership for Teacher Learning: Creating a culture where all teachers improve so that all students succeed*. West Palm Beach, FL: Learning Sciences International, 179–180.
294 Kennedy (2015).
295 Douglas, A. (n.d.). Mossbourne Habits [web page], http://bpmca.squarespace.com/planning#/mossbourne-habits/.
296 Fletcher-Wood, H. (2018). *Responsive Teaching: Cognitive science and formative assessment in practice*. Abingdon: Routledge.
297 Wiliam (2016), 175–176.
298 For a full discussion of exit tickets see Fletcher-Wood (2018), Ch. 4.
299 Bambrick-Santoyo (2016); Kraft, M. and Blazar, D. (2016). Individualized coaching to improve teacher practice across grades and subjects: New experimental evidence. *Educational Policy*, 31(7), 1033–1068.

300 Mountstevens, E. (2019). A little better all the time – 30th October 2019. Catalysing Learning [blog], https://catalysinglearning.wordpress.com/2019/10/30/a-little-better-all-the-time/.

301 Arnett, T., Moesta, B. and Horn, M.B. (2018). The teacher's quest for progress: How school leaders can motivate instructional innovation. Clayton Christensen Institute for Disruptive Innovation, 6.

302 Bellé, N. (2013). Leading to make a difference: A field experiment on the performance effects of transformational leadership, perceived social impact, and public service motivation. *Journal of Public Administration Research and Theory*, 24(1), 109–136.

303 Arnett, Moesta and Horn (2018), 4–5.

304 Kennedy (2015).

305 Kennedy, M. (2016). How does professional development improve teaching? *Review of Educational Research*, 86(4), 945–980.

306 Popp, J. and Goldman, S. (2016). Knowledge building in teacher professional learning communities: Focus of meeting matters. *Teaching and Teacher Education*, 59, 347–359; Supovitz, J. (2013). The linking study: An experiment to strengthen teachers' engagement with data on teaching and learning. CPRE Working Papers, https://repository.upenn.edu/cgi/viewcontent.cgi?article=1010&context=cpre_workingpapers.

307 Kennedy (2016).

308 Teacher Tapp (2018b). What Teachers Tapped this Week #63–10th December 2018. Teacher Tapp [blog], https://teachertapp.co.uk/2018/12/what-teachers-tapped-this-week-63-10th-december-2018/.

309 Behavioural Insights Team (2015), 34–38.

310 Ronfeldt, M. and Grossman, P. (2008). Becoming a professional: Experimenting with possible selves in professional preparation. *Teacher Education Quarterly*, 35(3), 41–60.

311 Gibson (2004).

312 Valente (1996).

313 For the effectiveness of instructional coaching, see Kraft, M., Blazar, D. and Hogan, D. (2018). The effect of teacher coaching on instruction and achievement: A meta-analysis of the causal evidence. *Review of Educational Research*, 88(4), 547–588; for commitments, see Bambrick-Santoyo (2016), 56–57. For the effectiveness of teacher learning communities, see Vescio, V., Ross, D. and Adams, A. (2007). A review of research on the impact of professional learning communities on teaching practice and student learning. *Teaching and Teacher Education*, 24, 80–91; for commitments, see Wiliam (2016), 175–176.

314 Wiliam (2016), 175–176.

315 Mountstevens (2019).

316 Odell, F. (2020). Term Time Well-being. When in Rome . . . – 4th January 2020 [blog], https://wheninromeeng.wordpress.com/2020/01/04/term-time-well-being/.

317 Grossman, P., Compton, C., Igra, D., Ronfeldt, M., Shahan, E. and Williamson, P. (2009). Teaching practice: A cross-professional perspective. *Teachers College Record*, 111(9), 2055–2100.

318 Cohen, J., Wong, V., Krishnamachari, A. and Berlin, R. (2020). Teacher coaching in a simulated environment. *Educational Evaluation and Policy Analysis*, 42(2), 208–231.

319 Binder (1996).

320 Grossman et al. (2009); Ericsson and Pool (2016).

321 Wiliam (2016), 175–176.

322 Mountstevens (2019).

323 For expense, see Wiliam (2016), 61; for limited effects, including for group rewards, see Fryer (2017); for an exception, which framed rewards as a potential loss, see Fryer, R., Levitt, S., List, J. and Sadoff, S. (2012). Enhancing the efficacy of teacher incentives through loss aversion: A field experiment. NBER Working Paper No. 18237.

324 Teacher Tapp (2018b).

325 Behavioural Insights Team (2015).

326 Bellé (2013); Grant, A. (2008). The significance of task significance: Job performance effects, relational mechanisms, and boundary conditions. *Journal of Applied Psychology*, 93(1), 108–124.

Resources

327 Sunstein and Reisch (2019).

328 Halpern (2015), 311.

329 Thaler, R. and Sunstein, C. (2008). *Nudge: Improving decisions about health, wealth and happiness.* London: Yale University Press.
330 Halpern (2015), 312.
331 Thaler and Sunstein (2008).
332 Ibid., 3.
333 Ibid.
334 Yeager and Walton (2011).
335 Cialdini (2007).
336 Halpern (2015), 332.

References

Aamodt, M. and McShane, T. (1992). A meta-analytic investigation of the effect of various test item characteristics on test scores and test completion times. *Public Personnel Management*, 21(2), 151–160.

Abrahamse, W. and Shwom, R. (2018). Domestic energy consumption and climate change mitigation. *WIREs Climate Change*, 9(14), e525.

Acland, D. and Levy, M.R. (2015). Naiveté, projection bias, and habit formation in gym attendance. *Management Science*, 61(1), 146–160.

Amabile, T. and Kramer, S. (2011). The power of small wins. *Harvard Business Review*. May.

Anderson, K. and Cavallaro, D. (2002) Parents or pop culture? Children's heroes and role models. *Childhood Education*, 78(3), 161–168.

Andrews, M. (2018). Implementing Public Policy: Is it possible to escape the "Public Policy Futility" trap? – 6th December 2018. Building State Capability [blog], https://buildingstatecapability.com/2018/12/06/implementing-public-policy-is-it-possible-to-escape-the-public-policy-futility-trap/.

Ariely, D. (2013). *The Honest Truth About Dishonesty: How we lie to everyone – especially ourselves.* London: Harper Perennial.

Ariely, D. and Wertenbroch, K. (2002). Procrastination, deadlines, and performance: Self-control by precommitment. *Psychological Science*, 13(3), 219–224.

Arnett, T., Moesta, B. and Horn, M.B. (2018). The teacher's quest for progress: How school leaders can motivate instructional innovation. Clayton Christensen Institute for Disruptive Innovation. Retrieved from https://www.christenseninstitute.org/wp-content/uploads/2018/08/JTBD.pdf.

Aronson, E. (1999). The power of self-persuasion. *American Psychologist*, 54(11), 875–884.

Atkins, M.S., McKay, M.M., Frazier, S.L., Jakobsons, L.J., Arvanitis, P., Cunningham, T., Brown, C. and Lambrecht, L. (2002). Suspensions and detentions in an urban, low-income school: Punishment or reward? *Journal of Abnormal Child Psychology*, 30(4), 361–371.

Austin, J., Sigurdsson, S. and Rubin, Y. (2006). An examination of the effects of delayed versus immediate prompts on safety belt use. *Environment and Behavior*, 38(1), 140–149.

Baars, S., Mulcahy, E. and Bernardes, E. (2016). The underrepresentation of white working class boys in higher education: The role of widening participation. London: LKMCo.

Bambrick-Santoyo, P. (2016) *Get Better Faster: A 90-day plan for coaching new teachers*. San Francisco: John Wiley and Sons.

Bandura, A. (1982). Self-efficacy mechanism in human agency. *American Psychologist*, 37(2), 122–147.

Barton, C. (2018). *How I Wish I'd Taught Maths: Lessons learned from research, conversations with experts, and 12 years of mistakes*. Woodbridge: John Catt.

Baumeister, R.F. and Leary, M.R. (1995). The need to belong: Desire for interpersonal attachments as a fundamental human motivation. *Psychological Bulletin*, 117(3), 497–529.

Behavioural Insights Team (2015). Behavioural Insights and the Somerset Challenge, https://www.bi.team/publications/behavioural-insights-and-the-somerset-challenge/.

Behavioural Insights Team (2019). Annual Report 2017-18. Behavioural Insights Team, https://www.bi.team/publications/the-behavioural-insights-team-annual-report-2017-18/.

Bellé, N. (2013). Leading to make a difference: A field experiment on the performance effects of transformational leadership, perceived social impact, and public service motivation. *Journal of Public Administration Research and Theory*, 24(1), 109–136.

Berliner, D. (1988). *The Development of Expertise in Pedagogy*. Charles W. Hunt Memorial Lecture presented at the Annual Meeting of the American Association of Colleges for Teacher Education (New Orleans, LA, February 17-20).

Bertrand, M., Mullainathan, S. and Shafir, E. (2006). Behavioral economics and marketing in aid of decision making among the poor. *Journal of Public Policy & Marketing*, 25(1), 8-23.

Binder, C. (1996). Behavioral fluency: Evolution of a new paradigm. *The Behavior Analyst*, 19(2), 163-197.

Bransford, J., Sherwood, R., Hasselbring, T., Klinzer, C. and Williams, S. (1990). Anchored instruction: Why we need it and how technology can help (Chapter 5). In D. Nix and R. Spiro (Eds.) *Cognition, Education, and Multimedia: Exploring ideas in high technology*. Hillsdale, NJ: Lawrence Erlbaum Associates, 117.

Briscese, G. and Tan, C. (2018). Applying Behavioural Insights to Labour Markets. Behavioural Insights Team, https://www.bi.team/publications/applying-behavioural-insights-to-labour-markets/.

Bryant, A.L. and Zimmerman, M.A. (2003). Role models and psychosocial outcomes among African American adolescents. *Journal of Adolescent Research*, 18(1), 36-67.

Burger, N., Charness, G. and Lynham, J. (2011). Field and online experiments on self-control. *Journal of Economic Behavior & Organization*, 77, 393-404.

Burger, N. and Lynham, J. (2010). Betting on weight loss . . . and losing: Personal gambles as commitment mechanisms. *Applied Economics Letters*, 17(12), 1161-1166.

Burgess, S. (2016) Michelle Obama and an English school: The power of inspiration, https://simonbur gesseconomics.co.uk/wp-content/uploads/2016/06/EGA-paper-20160627.pdf.

Bursztyn, L. and Jensen, R. (2015). How does peer pressure affect educational investments? *The Quarterly Journal of Economics*, 130(3), 1329-1367.

Canning, E. and Harackiewicz, J. (2015). Teach it, don't preach it: The differential effects of directly communicated and self-generated utility-value information. *Motivation Science*, 1(1), 47-71.

Caplan, B. (2018). *The Case Against Education: Why the education system is a waste of time and money*. Princeton, NJ: Princeton University Press, 135.

Castleman, B. and Page, L. (2015). Summer nudging: Can personalized text messages and peer mentor outreach increase college going among low-income high school graduates? *Journal of Economic Behavior & Organization*, 115, 144-160.

Charness, G. and Gneezy, U. (2009). Incentives to exercise. *Econometrica*, 77(3), 909-931.

Cialdini, R. (2007). *Influence: The psychology of persuasion*. New York: HarperBusiness.

Cialdini, R., Reno, R. and Kallgren, C. (1990). A focus theory of normative conduct: Recycling the concept of norms to reduce littering in public places. *Journal of Personality and Social Psychology*, 58(6), 1015-1026.

Clark, C., Osborne, S. and Dugdale, G. (2009). Reaching Out with Role Models: Role models and young people's reading. National Literacy Trust, https://literacytrust.org.uk/research-services/research-reports/reaching-out-role-models-role-models-and-young-peoples-reading-2009/.

Cohen, G.L., Garcia, J., Purdie-Vaughns, V., Apfel, N. and Brzustoski, P. (2009). Recursive processes in self-affirmation: Intervening to close the minority achievement gap. *Science*, 324(5925), 400-403.

Cohen, J., Wong, V., Krishnamachari, A. and Berlin, R. (2020). Teacher coaching in a simulated environment. *Educational Evaluation and Policy Analysis*, 42(2), 208-231.

Commonwealth of Australia (2018). Nudge vs Superbugs: A behavioural economics trial to reduce the overprescribing of antibiotics, https://www1.health.gov.au/internet/main/publishing.nsf/Content/Nudge-vs-Superbugs-behavioural-economics-trial-to-reduce-overprescribing-antibiotics-June-2018.

Cook, C., Fiat, A., Larson, M., Daikos, C., Slemrod, T., Holland, E., Thayer, A. and Renshaw, T. (2018). Positive greetings at the door: Evaluation of a low-cost, high-yield proactive classroom management strategy. *Journal of Positive Behavior Interventions*, 20(3), 149-159.

Dai, H., Milkman, K. and Riis, J. (2014). The fresh start effect: Temporal landmarks motivate aspirational behavior. *Management Science*, 60(10), 2563-2582.

Damgaard, M. and Nielsen, H. (2018). Nudging in education. *Economics of Education Review*, 64, 313-342.

de Wit, J., Das, E. and Vet, R. (2008). What works best: Objective statistics or a personal testimonial? An assessment of the persuasive effects of different types of message evidence on risk perception. *Health Psychology*, 27(1), 110-115.

Deutschman, A. (2005). Change or Die - 1st May 2005. Fast Company [blog], https://www.fastcompany.com/52717/change-or-die.

Didau, D. (2018). Teaching matters, but there are more important things to get right - 8th July 2018. Learning Spy [blog], https://learningspy.co.uk/featured/teaching-maters-but-there-are-more-important-things-to-get-right/.

Douglas, A. (n.d.). Mossbourne Habits [web page], http://bpmca.squarespace.com/planning#/mossbourne-habits/.

Duckworth, A.L., Kirby, T.A., Gollwitzer, A. and Oettingen, G. (2013). From fantasy to action: Mental contrasting with implementation intentions (MCII) improves academic performance in children. *Social Psychological and Personality Science*, 4(6), 745-753.

Duhigg, C. (2012) *The Power of Habit: Why we do what we do in life and business*. New York: Random House.

Dunlosky, J., Rawson, K., Marsh, E., Mitchell, J. and Willingham, D. (2013). Improving students' learning with effective learning techniques: Promising directions from cognitive and educational psychology. *Psychological Science in the Public Interest*, 14(1), 4-58.

Durantini, M., Albarracín, D., Mitchell, A., Earl, A. and Gillette, J. (2006). Conceptualizing the influence of social agents of behavior change: A meta-analysis of the effectiveness of HIV-prevention interventionists for different groups. *Psychological Bulletin*, 132(2), 212-248.

Elmore, R. (1996). Getting to scale with good educational practice. *Harvard Educational Review*, 66(1), 1-26.

Epton, T., Currie, S. and Armitage, C.J. (2017). Unique effects of setting goals on behavior change: Systematic review and meta-analysis. *Journal of Consulting and Clinical Psychology*, 85(12), 1182-1198.

Epton, T., Harris, P.R., Kane, R., van Koningsbruggen, G.M. and Sheeran, P. (2015). The impact of self-affirmation on health-behavior change: A meta-analysis. *Health Psychology*, 34(3), 187-196.

Ericsson, A. and Pool, R. (2016). *Peak: Secrets from the new science of expertise*. London: Bodley Head.

Ferraro, P.J., Miranda, J.J. and Price, M.K. (2011). The persistence of treatment effects with norm-based policy instruments: Evidence from a randomized environmental policy experiment. *American Economic Review*, 101(3), 318-322.

Fiorella, L. (2020). The science of habit and its implications for student learning and well-being. *Educational Psychology Review*, 32, 603-625.

Fisher, D., Frey, N. and Lapp, D. (2011a). Coaching middle-level teachers to think aloud improves comprehension instruction and student reading achievement. *The Teacher Educator*, 46(3), 231-243.

Fisher, D., Frey, N. and Lapp, D. (2011b). Focusing on the participation and engagement gap: A case study on closing the achievement gap. *Journal of Education for Students Placed at Risk*, 16(1), 56-64.

Fletcher-Wood, H. (2016). *Ticked Off: Checklists for students, teachers and school leaders*. Bancyfelin: Crown House.

Fletcher-Wood, H. (2018). *Responsive Teaching: Cognitive science and formative assessment in practice*. Abingdon: Routledge.

Fryer, R.G. (2011). Financial incentives and student achievement: Evidence from randomized trials. *The Quarterly Journal of Economics*, 126(4), 1755-1798.

Fryer, R.G. (2017). The production of human capital in developed countries: Evidence from 196 randomized field experiments. In E. Duflo and A. Banerjee (Eds.) *Handbook of Economic Field Experiments* (Vol. 2). Amsterdam: North-Holland, 95-322.

Fryer, R., Levitt, S., List, J. and Sadoff, S. (2012). Enhancing the efficacy of teacher incentives through loss aversion: A field experiment. NBER Working Paper No. 18237.

Gardner, B. (2014). A review and analysis of the use of "habit" in understanding, predicting and influencing health-related behaviour. *Health Psychology Review*, 9(3), 277-295.

Garon-Carrier, G., Boivin, M., Guay, F., Kovas, Y., Dionne, G., Lemelin, J.P., Séguin, J.R., Vitaro, F. and Tremblay, R.E. (2016). Intrinsic motivation and achievement in mathematics in elementary school: A longitudinal investigation of their association. *Child Development*, 87(1), 165-175.

Gawande, A. (2010). *The Checklist Manifesto: How to get things right*. London: Profile.

Gehlbach, H., Brinkworth, M.E., King, A.M., Hsu, L.M., McIntyre, J. and Rogers, T. (2016). Creating birds of similar feathers: Leveraging similarity to improve teacher–student relationships and academic achievement. *Journal of Educational Psychology*, 108(3), 342-352.

Gibson, D. (2004). Role models in career development: New directions for theory and research. *Journal of Vocational Behaviour*, 65(1), 134-156.

Gilovich, T., Kerr, M. and Medvec, V. (1993). Effect of temporal perspective on subjective confidence. *Journal of Personality and Social Psychology*, 64(4), 552-560.

Giné, X., Karlan, D. and Zinman, J. (2010). Put your money where your butt is: A commitment contract for smoking cessation. *American Economic Journal: Applied Economics*, 2(4), 213-235.

Gneezy, U., Meier, S. and Rey-Biel, P. (2011). When and why incentives (don't) work to modify behavior. *The Journal of Economic Perspectives*, 25(4), 191-209.

Gollwitzer, P. and Sheeran, P. (2006). Implementation intentions and goal achievement: A meta-analysis of effects and processes. *Advances in Experimental Social Psychology*, 38, 69-119.

Grant, A. (2008). The significance of task significance: Job performance effects, relational mechanisms, and boundary conditions. *Journal of Applied Psychology*, 93(1), 108 -124.

Groot, B., Sanders, M., Rogers, T. and Bloomenthal, E. (2017). I get by with a little help from my friends: Two field experiments on social support and attendance in further education colleges in the UK. Behavioural Insights Team, https://www.behaviouralinsights.co.uk/wp-content/uploads/2017/06/Study-Supporter-Working-Paper_2017.pdf.

Grossman, P., Compton, C., Igra, D., Ronfeldt, M., Shahan, E. and Williamson, P. (2009). Teaching practice: A cross-professional perspective. *Teachers College Record*, 111(9), 2055-2100.

Haidt, J. (2013). *The Righteous Mind: Why good people are divided by politics and religion*. London: Penguin.

Haidt, J., Seder, J.P. and Kesebir, S. (2008). Hive psychology, happiness, and public policy. *The Journal of Legal Studies*, 37(S2), S133-S156.

Halpern, D. (2015). *Inside the Nudge Unit: How small changes can make a big difference*. London: WH Allen.

Hand, E. (2016). No pressure: NSF test finds eliminating deadlines halves number of grant proposals. *Science*. 15th April, https://www.sciencemag.org/news/2016/04/no-pressure-nsf-test-finds-eliminating-deadlines-halves-number-grant-proposals#.

Harford, T. (2019). Lunch with the FT. Richard Thaler: "If you want people to do something, make it easy." *Financial Times*, 2nd August.

Hawton, K., Simkin, S., Dodd, S., Pocock, P., Bernal, W., Gunnell, D. and Kapur, N. (2013). Long term effect of reduced pack sizes of paracetamol on poisoning deaths and liver transplant activity in England and Wales: Interrupted time series analyses. *British Medical Journal*, 346, f403.

Haydn, T. (2014). To what extent is behaviour a problem in English schools? Exploring the scale and prevalence of deficits in classroom climate. *Review of Education*, 2(1), 31-64.

Heath, C. and Heath, D. (2010). *Switch: How to change things when change is hard*. London: Random House.

Heath, C. and Heath, D. (2017). *The Power of Moments: Why certain experiences have extraordinary impact*. New York: Simon and Schuster.

Hershfield, H.E., Goldstein, D.G., Sharpe, W.F., Fox, J., Yeykelis, L., Carstensen, L.L. and Bailenson, J.N. (2011). Increasing saving behavior through age-progressed renderings of the future self. *Journal of Marketing Research*, 48(SPL), S23-S37.

House, B. (2017). How do social norms influence prosocial development? *Current Opinion in Psychology*, 20, 87-91.

Hulleman, C. and Harackiewicz, J. (2009). Promoting interest and performance in high school science classes. *Science*, 326(5958), 1410-1412.

Hume, S., O'Reilly, F., Groot, B., Chande, R., Sanders, M., Hollingsworth, A., Ter Meer, J., Barnes, J., Booth, S., Kozman, E. and Soon, X. (2018). Improving engagement and attainment in maths and English courses: Insights from behavioural research: Research and project report. Department for Education, https://www.gov.uk/government/publications/improving-engagement-and-attainment-in-maths-and-english-courses.

Isaac, A. (2018). Auto-enrolment pensions are a hit – with one major catch. *The Daily Telegraph*, 8th May, https://www.telegraph.co.uk/business/2018/05/08/auto-enrolment-pensions-hit-one-major-catch/.

Jalava, N., Joensen, J.S. and Pellas, E. (2015). Grades and rank: Impacts of non-financial incentives on test performance. *Journal of Economic Behavior & Organization*, 115, 161-196.

Kahan, D. (2000). Gentle nudges vs. hard shoves: Solving the sticky norms problem. *The University of Chicago Law Review*, 67(3), 607-645.

Kahneman, D. (2011). *Thinking, fast and slow*. London: Penguin.

Kahneman, D., Knetsch, J.L. and Thaler, R.H. (1991). Anomalies: The endowment effect, loss aversion, and status quo bias. *Journal of Economic Perspectives*, 5(1), 193-206.

Kaushal, N. and Rhodes, R. (2015). Exercise habit formation in new gym members: A longitudinal study. *Journal of Behavioral Medicine*, 38, 652-663.

Keizer, K., Lindenburg, S. and Steg, L. (2008). The spreading of disorder. *Science*, 322(5908), 1681–1685.

Keller, P., Harlam, B., Loewenstein, G. and Volpp, K. (2011). Enhanced active choice: A new method to motivate behavior change. *Journal of Consumer Psychology*, 21, 376–383.

Kennedy, M. (2010). Attribution error and the quest for teacher quality. *Educational Researcher*, 39(8), 591–598.

Kennedy, M. (2015). Parsing the practice of teaching. *Journal of Teacher Education*, 67(1), 6–17.

Kennedy, M. (2016). How does professional development improve teaching? *Review of Educational Research*, 86(4), 945–980.

Kirschner, P. and van Merriënboer, J. (2013). Do learners really know best? Urban legends in education. *Educational Psychologist*, 48(3), 169–183.

Klein, R., Vianello, M., Hasselman, F., Adams, B., Adams, R., Alper, S., Aveyard, M., Kappes, H., et al. (2018). Many labs 2: Investigating variation in replicability across sample and setting. *Advances in Methods and Practices in Psychological Science*, 1(4), 443–490.

Kniveton, B. (2004). The influences and motivations on which students base their choice of career. *Research in Education*, 72, 47–57.

Kraft, M. and Blazar, D. (2016). Individualized coaching to improve teacher practice across grades and subjects: New experimental evidence. *Educational Policy*, 31(7), 1033–1068.

Kraft, M., Blazar, D. and Hogan, D. (2018). The effect of teacher coaching on instruction and achievement: A meta-analysis of the causal evidence. *Review of Educational Research*, 88(4), 547–588.

Kruger, J. and Dunning, D. (1999). Unskilled and unaware of it: How difficulties in recognizing one's own incompetence lead to inflated self-assessments. *Journal of Personality and Social Psychology*, 77(6), 1121–1134.

Kuhberger, A. (1998). The influence of framing on risky decisions: A meta-analysis. *Organizational Behavior and Human Decision Processes*, 75(1), 23–55.

Lally, P. and Gardner, B. (2013). Promoting habit formation. *Health Psychology Review*, 7(sup1), S137–S158.

Lally, P., van Jaarsveld, C., Potts, H. and Wardle, J. (2010). How are habits formed: Modelling habit formation in the real world. *European Journal of Social Psychology*, 40(6), 998–1009.

Larkin, J., McDermott, J., Simon, D. and Simon, H. (1980). Expert and novice performance in solving physics problems. *Science*, 208(4450), 1335–1342.

Lavecchia, A.M., Liu, H. and Oreopoulos, P. (2016). Behavioral economics of education: Progress and possibilities. In Eric A. Hanushek, Stephen Machin and Ludger Woessmann (eds) *Handbook of the Economics of Education* (Vol. 5). Amsterdam: Elsevier, 1–74.

Lemov, D. (2015a). *Teach Like a Champion 2.0*. San Francisco: Jossey-Bass.

Lemov, D. (2015b). Hunting versus fishing – 24th July 2015. Teach Like a Champion [blog], https://teachlikeachampion.com/blog/hunting-versus-fishing/.

Lemov, D., Woolway, E. and Yezzi, K. (2012). *Practice Perfect: 42 rules for getting better at getting better*. San Francisco: Jossey-Bass.

Lepper, M., Henderlong Corpus, J. and Iyengar, S. (2005). Intrinsic and extrinsic motivational orientations in the classroom: Age differences and academic correlates. *Journal of Educational Psychology*, 97(2), 184–196.

Leventhal, H., Singer, R. and Jones, S. (1965). Effects of fear and specificity of recommendation upon attitudes and behavior. *Journal of Personality and Social Psychology*, 2(1), 20–29.

Levitt, S.D., List, J.A., Neckermann, S. and Sadoff, S. (2016). The behavioralist goes to school: Leveraging behavioral economics to improve educational performance. *American Economic Journal: Economic Policy*, 8(4), 183–219.

Lin-Siegler, X., Ahn, J.N., Chen, J., Fang, F.F.A. and Luna-Lucero, M. (2016). Even Einstein struggled: Effects of learning about great scientists' struggles on high school students' motivation to learn science. *Journal of Educational Psychology*, 108(3), 314–328.

Locke, E.A. and Latham, G.P. (2002). Building a practically useful theory of goal setting and task motivation. *American Psychologist*, 57(9), 705–717.

Lockwood, P. and Kunda, Z. (1997). Superstars and me: Predicting the impact of role models on the self. *Journal of Personality and Social Psychology*, 73(1), 91–103.

Lovell, O. (2018a). When the space, retrieve, interleave formula doesn't work! – 2nd April 2018. ollielovell.com [blog], http://www.ollielovell.com/olliesclassroom/fail-v1/.

Lovell, O. (2018b). Implementation Intentions and action triggers: Moving beyond "Well, make sure you do it next time" – 15th November 2018. ollielovell.com [blog], http://www.ollielovell.com/olliesclassroom/implementation-intentions-action-triggers/.

Macnamara, B.N., Hambrick, D.Z., Frank, D.J., King, M.J., Burgoyne, A.P. and Meinz, E.J. (2018). The deliberate practice view: An evaluation of definitions, claims, and empirical evidence (Ch. 9). In D.Z. Hambrick, G. Campitelli and B.N. Macnamara (Eds.) *The Science of Expertise: Behavioral, neural, and genetic approaches to complex skill*. Abingdon: Routledge.

Mayer, R. (2004). Should there be a three-strikes rule against pure discovery learning? The case for guided methods of instruction. *American Psychologist*, 59(1), 14–19.

McCrea, E. (2019). *Making Every Maths Lesson Count: Six principles to support great maths teaching*. Bancyfelin: Crown House.

McGaghie, W.C., Issenberg, S.B., Cohen, M.E.R., Barsuk, J.H. and Wayne, D.B. (2011). Does simulation-based medical education with deliberate practice yield better results than traditional clinical education? A meta-analytic comparative review of the evidence. *Academic Medicine: Journal of the Association of American Medical Colleges*, 86(6), 706–711.

McInerney, L. (2012). Ms McInerney's "Book of Consequences" Detention System – 17th November 2012. LauraMcinerney.com [blog], https://lauramcinerney.com/ms-mcinerneys-book-of-consequences-detention-system/.

Maruna, S. (2011). Reentry as a rite of passage. *Punishment & Society*, 13(1), 3–28.

Meyer, D. (2015). "If Math Is The Aspirin, Then How Do You Create The Headache?" – 17th June 2015. mrmeyer.com [blog], https://blog.mrmeyer.com/2015/if-math-is-the-aspirin-then-how-do-you-create-the-headache/.

Meyer, D. (n.d.) Directory of Mathematical Headaches. https://docs.google.com/document/d/1JZmjliqJik VD69y5ZY8wOV8MI47lBdH1DrhLiBeKQh8/edit.

Milkman, K. and Riis, J. (2014). The fresh start effect: Temporal landmarks motivate aspirational behavior. *Management Science*, 60(10), 2563–2582.

Milkman, K.L., Beshears, J., Choi, J.J., Laibson, D. and Madrian, B.C. (2011). Using implementation intentions prompts to enhance influenza vaccination rates. *Proceedings of the National Academy of Sciences*, 108(26), 10415–10420.

Milkman, K., Minson, J. and Volpp, K. (2014). Holding the Hunger Games hostage at the gym: An evaluation of temptation bundling. *Management Science*, 60(2), 283–299.

Miller, S., Davison, J., Yohanis, J., Sloan, S., Gildea, A. and Thurston, A. (2016). Texting parents: Evaluation report and executive summary. Education Endowment Fund, https://educationendowmentfoundation.org.uk/projects-and-evaluation/projects/texting-parents/.

Mook, D. (1983). In defense of external invalidity. *American Psychologist*, 38(4), 379–387.

Mountstevens, E. (2019). A little better all the time – 30th October 2019. Catalysing Learning [blog], https://catalysinglearning.wordpress.com/2019/10/30/a-little-better-all-the-time/.

Nelson, M. and Schunn, C. (2008). The nature of feedback: How different types of peer feedback affect writing performance. *Instructional Science*, 37(4), 375–401.

Nosek, B., Cohoon, J., Kidwell, M. and Spies, J. (2015). Estimating the reproducibility of psychological science. *Science*, 349(6251).

Nunes, J. and Dreze, X. (2006). The endowed progress effect: How artificial advancement increases effort. *Journal of Consumer Research*, 32(4), 504–512.

Nuthall, G. (2005). The cultural myths and realities of classroom teaching and learning: A personal journey. *Teachers College Record*, 107(5), 895–934.

Nuthall, G. (2007). *The Hidden Lives of Learners*. Wellington: New Zealand Council for Educational Research.

Nyer, P. and Dellande, S. (2010). Public commitment as a motivator for weight loss. *Psychology & Marketing*, 27(1), 1–12.

Odell, F. (2020). Term Time Well-being. When in Rome . . . – 4th January 2020 [blog], https://wheninromeeng.wordpress.com/2020/01/04/term-time-well-being/.

Paluck, E.L. (2009). Reducing intergroup prejudice and conflict using the media: A field experiment in Rwanda. *Journal of Personality and Social Psychology*, 96(3), 574–587.

Panadero, E., Jonsson, A. and Botella, J. (2017). Effects of self-assessment on self-regulated learning and self-efficacy: Four meta-analyses. *Educational Research Review*, 22, 74–98.

Pichert, D. and Katsikopoulos, K. (2008). Green defaults: Information presentation and pro-environmental behaviour. *Journal of Environmental Psychology*, 28, 63–73.

Pink, D. (2018). *When: The scientific secrets of perfect timing*. Edinburgh: Canongate.

Popp, J. and Goldman, S. (2016). Knowledge building in teacher professional learning communities: Focus of meeting matters. *Teaching and Teacher Education*, 59, 347–359.

Read, D., Loewenstein, G. and Kalyanarman, S. (1999). Mixing virtue and vice: Combining the immediacy effect and the diversification heuristic. *Journal of Behavioral Decision Making*, 12, 257-273.

Recht, D.R. and Leslie, L. (1988). Effect of prior knowledge on good and poor readers' memory of text. *Journal of Educational Psychology*, 80, 16-20.

Renkl, A., Hilbert, T. and Schworm, S. (2009). Example-based learning in heuristic domains: A cognitive load theory account. *Educational Psychology Review*, 21(1), 67-78.

Rogers, T. and Feller, A. (2016). Discouraged by peer excellence: Exposure to exemplary peer performance causes quitting. *Psychological Science*, 27(3), 365-374.

Rogers, T. and Feller, A. (2018). Reducing student absences at scale by targeting parents' misbeliefs. *Nature Human Behaviour*, 2(5), 335-342.

Rogers, T., Milkman, K., John, L. and Norton, M. (2015). Beyond good intentions: Prompting people to make plans improves follow-through on important tasks. *Behavioral Science & Policy*, 1(2), 33-41.

Ronfeldt, M. and Grossman, P. (2008). Becoming a professional: Experimenting with possible selves in professional preparation. *Teacher Education Quarterly*, 35(3), 41-60.

Rothman, A., Bartels, R., Wlaschin, J. and Salovey, P. (2006). The strategic use of gain- and loss-framed messages to promote healthy behavior: How theory can inform practice. *Journal of Communications* (56), S202-S220.

Ryan, R. and Deci, E. (2000). Self-determination theory and the facilitation of intrinsic motivation, social development, and well-being. *American Psychologist*, 55(1), 68-78.

Sacerdote, B. (2001). Peer effects with random assignment: Results for Dartmouth roommates. *The Quarterly Journal of Economics*, 116(2), 681-704.

Sadler, D. (1989). Formative assessment and the design of instructional systems. *Instructional Science*, 18(2), 119-144.

Sanders, M., Chonaire, A.N., Carr, D., Heal, J. and Anik, L. (2017). Increasing Social Trust with an Ice-Breaking Exercise: An RCT Carried out with NCS participants. Behavioural Insights Team. http://www.behaviouralinsights.co.uk/wp-content/uploads/2017/03/Increasing-social-trust.pdf.

Scandone, B., Wishart, R., Griggs, J., Smith, N., Burridge, H., Lepanjuuri, K., Hall, P., Chadwick, T. and Averill, P. (2020). Texting students and study supporters (Project SUCCESS). Education Endowment Foundation, https://educationendowmentfoundation.org.uk/projects-and-evaluation/projects/texting-students-and-study-supporters/.

Service, O., Hallsworth, M., Halpern, D., Algate, F., Gallagher, R., Nguyen, S., Ruda, S. and Sanders, M. (2014). EAST: Four simple ways to apply behavioural insights. Behavioural Insights Team, https://www.bi.team/publications/east-four-simple-ways-to-apply-behavioural-insights/.

Sibieta, L., Greaves, E. and Sianesi, B. (2014). Increasing pupil motivation: Evaluation report and executive summary. Education Endowment Foundation, https://educationendowmentfoundation.org.uk/projects-and-evaluation/projects/increasing-pupil-motivation/.

Siegle, D. and McCoach, B. (2007). Increasing student mathematics self-efficacy through teacher training. *Journal of Advanced Academics*, 18(2), 278-312.

Silkwood School (n.d.). Moments that Matter [web page], https://www.silkwood.qld.edu.au/silkwood-way/festivals-transition-ceremonies-and-camps.

Sims, S., Hobbiss, M. and Allen, R. (2020). Habit formation limits growth in teacher effectiveness: A review of converging evidence from neuroscience and social science. *Review of Education*, 9(1), 3-23.

Soderstrom, N. and Bjork, R. (2015). Learning versus performance: An integrative review. *Perspectives on Psychological Science*, 10(2), 176-199.

Sparkman, G. and Walton, G.M. (2017). Dynamic norms promote sustainable behavior, even if it is counternormative. *Psychological Science*, 28(11), 1663-1674.

Springer, M.G., Rosenquist, B.A. and Swain, W.A. (2015). Monetary and nonmonetary student incentives for tutoring services: A randomized controlled trial. *Journal of Research on Educational Effectiveness*, 8(4), 453-474.

Sunstein, A.R. and Reisch, L.A. (2019). *Trusting Nudges: Towards a bill of rights for nudging*. Abingdon: Routledge.

Supovitz, J. (2013). The linking study: An experiment to strengthen teachers' engagement with data on teaching and learning. CPRE Working Papers, https://repository.upenn.edu/cgi/viewcontent.cgi?article=1010&context=cpre_workingpapers.

Sweller, J. (1988). Cognitive load during problem solving: Effects on learning. *Cognitive Science*, 12(2), 257-285.

Sweller, J., Ayres, P.L., Kalyuga, S. and Chandler, P.A. (2003). The expertise reversal effect. *Educational Psychologist*, 38(1), 23-31.

Sweller, J., van Merriënboer J.J. and Paas F.G. (1998). Cognitive architecture and instructional design. *Educational Psychology Review*, 10, 251-296.

Taleb, N. (2018) *Skin in the Game: Hidden asymmetries in daily life*. London: Allen Lane.

Teacher Tapp (2018a). What Teachers Tapped This Week #62 – 3rd December 2018. Teacher Tapp [blog], http://teachertapp.co.uk/2018/12/what-teachers-tapped-this-week-62-3rd-december-2018/.

Teacher Tapp (2018b). What Teachers Tapped This Week #63 – 10th December 2018. Teacher Tapp [blog], https://teachertapp.co.uk/2018/12/what-teachers-tapped-this-week-63-10th-december-2018/.

Teacher Tapp (2019). Behaviour: What is going on in schools? (And how does it affect teachers?) – 10th February 2019. Teacher Tapp [blog], https://teachertapp.co.uk/2019/02/behaviour-what-is-really-going-on-in-schools-2019/.

Thaler, R. and Benartzi, S. (2004). Save more tomorrow: Using behavioral economics to increase employee saving. *Journal of Political Economy*, 112(1), 164-187.

Thaler, R. and Sunstein, C. (2008). *Nudge: Improving decisions about health, wealth and happiness*. London: Yale University Press.

Thompson, S., Michaelson, J., Abdallah, S., Johnson, V., Morris, D., Riley, K. and Simms, A. (2011). "Moments of change" as opportunities for influencing behaviour: A report to the Department for Environment, Food and Rural Affairs. London: Defra.

Todd, A. and Galinsky, A. (2014). Perspective-taking as a strategy for improving intergroup relations: Evidence, mechanisms, and qualifications. *Social and Personality Psychology Compass*, 8(7), 374-387.

Tu, Y. and Soman, D. (2014). The categorization of time and its impact on task initiation. *Journal of Consumer Research*, 41(3), 810-822.

Tze, V.M., Daniels, L.M. and Klassen, R.M. (2016). Evaluating the relationship between boredom and academic outcomes: A meta-analysis. *Educational Psychology Review*, 28(1), 119-144.

Valente, T. (1996). Social network thresholds in the diffusion of innovations. *Social Networks*, 18(1), 69-89.

van Bergen, E., Snowling, M.J., de Zeeuw, E.L., van Beijsterveldt, C.E., Dolan, C.V. and Boomsma, D.I. (2018). Why do children read more? The influence of reading ability on voluntary reading practices. *Journal of Child Psychology and Psychiatry*, 59(11), 1205-1214.

van Merriënboer, J., Kester, L. and Paas, F. (2006). Teaching complex rather than simple tasks: Balancing intrinsic and germane load to enhance transfer of learning. *Applied Cognitive Psychology*, 20(3), 343-352.

Verplanken, B. and Wood, W. (2006). Interventions to break and create consumer habits. *Journal of Public Policy & Marketing*, 25(1), 90-103.

Vescio, V., Ross, D. and Adams, A. (2007). A review of research on the impact of professional learning communities on teaching practice and student learning. *Teaching and Teacher Education*, 24, 80-91.

Walton, G.M., Cohen, G.L., Cwir, D. and Spencer, S.J. (2012). Mere belonging: The power of social connections. *Journal of Personality and Social Psychology*, 102(3), 513-532.

Webb, T. and Sheeran, P. (2006). Does changing behavioral intentions engender behavior change? A meta-analysis of the experimental evidence. *Psychological Bulletin*, 132(2), 249-268.

Webb, T., Sheeran, P. and Luszczynska, A. (2009). Planning to break unwanted habits: Habit strength moderates implementation intention effects on behaviour change. *British Journal of Social Psychology*, 48, 507-523.

Wiliam, D. (2016). *Leadership for Teacher Learning: Creating a culture where all teachers improve so that all students succeed*. West Palm Beach, FL: Learning Sciences International, 179-180.

Willingham, D. (2009). *Why Don't Students Like School? A cognitive scientist answers questions about how the mind works and what it means for the classroom*. San Francisco, CA: Jossey-Bass.

Wood, W. and Neal, D. (2007). A new look at habits and the habit-goal interface. *Psychological Review*, 114(4), 843-863.

Wood, W. and Neal, D. (2016). Healthy through habit: Interventions for initiating & maintaining health behavior change. *Behavioral Science & Policy*, 2(1), 71-83.

Wood, W., Quinn, J. and Kashy, D. (2002). Habits in everyday life: Thought, emotion, and action. *Journal of Personality and Social Psychology*, 83(6), 1281-1297.

Worchel, S. (1992). Beyond a commodity theory analysis of censorship: When abundance and personalism enhance scarcity effects. *Basic and Applied Social Psychology*, 13(1), 79-92.

Worth, J. and Van den Brande, J. (2020). Teacher autonomy: How does it relate to job satisfaction and retention? NFER, https://www.nfer.ac.uk/teacher-autonomy-how-does-it-relate-to-job-satisfaction-and-retention/.

Yeager, D. and Walton, G. (2011). Social-psychological interventions in education: They're not magic. *Review of Educational Research*, 81(2), 267–301.

Yeager, D.S., Henderson, M.D., Paunesku, D., Walton, G.M., D'Mello, S., Spitzer, B.J. and Duckworth, A.L. (2014). Boring but important: A self-transcendent purpose for learning fosters academic self-regulation. *Journal of Personality and Social Psychology*, 107(4), 559–580.

Yeager, D., Purdie-Vaughns, V., Garcia, J., Apfel, N., Brzustoski, P., Master, A., Hessert, W., Williams, M. and Cohen, G. (2014). Breaking the cycle of mistrust: Wise interventions to provide critical feedback across the racial divide. *Journal of Experimental Psychology: General*, 143(2), 804–824.

Zimmerman, B. (2002). Becoming a self-regulated learner: An overview. *Theory Into Practice*, 41(2), 64–70.

Index

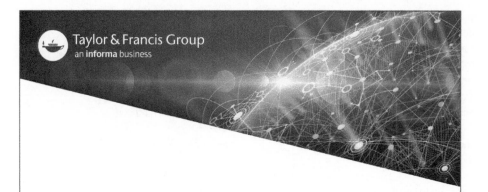

Taylor & Francis Group
an **informa** business

Taylor & Francis eBooks

www.taylorfrancis.com

A single destination for eBooks from Taylor & Francis
with increased functionality and an improved user
experience to meet the needs of our customers.

90,000+ eBooks of award-winning academic content in
Humanities, Social Science, Science, Technology, Engineering,
and Medical written by a global network of editors and authors.

TAYLOR & FRANCIS EBOOKS OFFERS:

A streamlined
experience for
our library
customers

A single point
of discovery
for all of our
eBook content

Improved
search and
discovery of
content at both
book and
chapter level

REQUEST A FREE TRIAL
support@taylorfrancis.com

 Routledge
Taylor & Francis Group

 CRC Press
Taylor & Francis Group